CINDER

Also by SUSAN STEWART

POETRY

Yellow Stars and Ice
The Hive
The Forest
The Elements
Columbarium
Red Rover

PROSE

Nonsense
On Longing
Crimes of Writing
Poetry and the Fate of the Senses
The Open Studio
The Poet's Freedom

TRANSLATIONS

Euripides, *Andromache* (with Wesley D. Smith)
Alda Merini, *Love Lessons: Selected Poems*
Milo De Angelis, *Theme of Farewell and After-Poems* (with Patrizio Ceccagnoli)
Laudomia Bonanni, *The Reprisal* (with Sara Teardo)

CINDER

New and Selected Poems

SUSAN STEWART

Graywolf Press

Poems from *The Forest, Columbarium,* and *Red Rover* published with the permission of the University of Chicago Press. Poems from *The Hive* published with the permission of the University of Georgia Press. Poems from *Yellow Stars and Ice* published with the permission of Princeton University Press.

This publication is made possible, in part, by the voters of Minnesota through a Minnesota State Arts Board Operating Support grant, thanks to a legislative appropriation from the arts and cultural heritage fund, and through a grant from the Wells Fargo Foundation. Significant support has also been provided by Target, the McKnight Foundation, the Lannan Foundation, the Amazon Literary Partnership, and other generous contributions from foundations, corporations, and individuals. To these organizations and individuals we offer our heartfelt thanks.

This book is made possible through a partnership with the College of Saint Benedict, and honors the legacy of S. Mariella Gable, a distinguished teacher at the College. Support has been provided by the Manitou Fund as part of the Warner Reading Program.

Special funding for this title was provided by Edwin C. Cohen.

Published by Graywolf Press
250 Third Avenue North, Suite 600
Minneapolis, Minnesota 55401

www.graywolfpress.org

Published in the United States of America

ISBN 978-1-55597-763-4 (cloth)
ISBN 978-1-55597-795-5 (paper)

2 4 6 8 9 7 5 3 1
First Graywolf Paperback, 2018

Library of Congress Control Number: 2017937996

Cover design: Jeenee Lee Design

Cover illustrations: Tim Horton (front) and Ann Hamilton (back). Grass image licensed under the Creative Commons Attribution-Share Alike 2.5 Generic license. The orientation, color, and clarity of the original image have been altered. Twine image courtesy of the Ann Hamilton Studio. With thanks to Ann Hamilton for her assistance.

Contents

CINDER

Pine: New Poems
(2009–2015)

Field in Winter

The world, a museum of itself.

The cold colonnade of dying elms.

You cannot will a dream, though you, too,

can fall, and fall asleep, and wake

in wonder. There is nowhere

the whiteness has not

touched—take

    a look and

see. The corners, the edge, of each

thing exposed:

you walked into a new transparency,

Pine

a homely word:
a plosive, a long cry, a quiet stop, a silent letter
      like a storm and the end of a storm,
the kind brewing
      at the top of a pine,
          (torn hair, bowed spirits and,
              later, straightened shoulders)
who's who of the stirred and stirred up:
      musicians, revolutionaries, pines.

A coniferous tree with needle-shaped leaves.
Suffering or trouble; there's a pin inside.

The aphoristic seamstress was putting up a hem, a shelf of pins at her pursed mouth.
"needles and pins / needles and pins / when a man marries / his trouble begins."
A red pincushion with a twisted string, and a little pinecone tassel, at the ready.

That particular smell, bracing,
      exact as a sharpened point.

The Christmas tree, nude and fragrant,
      propped as pure potential in
the corner with no nostalgia for
      ornament or angels.

"Pine-Sol," nauseating, earnest, imitation—

        one means of knowing the real thing is the fake you find in school.

Pent up inside on a winter day, the steaming closeness from the radiators.

At the bell, running down the hillside. You wore a pinafore.

The air had a nip: pine

        was traveling in the opposite direction.

Sunlight streaming through a stand of pines,

        dancing backward through the A's and T's.

Is it fern or willow that's the opposite of pine?

An alphabet made of trees.

In the clearing vanished hunters

        left their arrowheads

        and deep cuts in the boulder wall:

            petroglyphs, repeating triangles.

Grandmothers wearing pinnies trimmed in rickrack.

One family branch lived in a square of oak forest, the other in a circle of pines;

        the oak line: solid, reliable, comic; the piney one capable of pain and surprise.

W-H-I-T-E: the white pine's five-frond sets spell its name. (Orthography of other pines

        I don't yet know.)

The weight of snow on boughs, lethargic, then rocked by the thump of a settling crow.

Pine cones at the Villa Borghese: Fibonacci increments,

      heart-shaped veins, shadowing the inner

           edges of the petals.

Like variations at the margins of a bird feather.

      Graffiti tattooing the broken

         water clock, a handful

              of pine nuts, pried out, for lunch.

Pining away like Respighi with your pencil.

For a coffin, you'd pick a plain

pine box suspended in a weedy sea.

No undergrowth, though, in a pine forest.

Unlike the noisy wash

of dry deciduous leaves,

the needles blanket the earth

pliant beneath a bare foot,

stealthy,

       floating,

a walk through the pines.

Silence in the forest comes from hooks.

A Language

       I had heard the story before
about the two prisoners, alone
in the same cell, and one
gives the other lessons in a language.

Day after day, the pupil studies hard—
what else does he have to do?—and year
after year they practice,
waiting for the hour of release.

They tackle the nouns, the cases, and genders,
the rules for imperatives and conjugations,
but near the end of his sentence, the teacher
suddenly dies and only the pupil
goes back through the gate and into the open
world. He travels to the country of his new
language, fluent, and full of hope.

Yet when he arrives he finds
that the language he speaks is not
the language that is spoken. He has learned
a language one other person knew—its inventor,
his cell-mate and teacher.

       And then the other
evening, I heard the story again.
This time the teacher was Gombrowicz, the pupil
was his wife. She had dreamed of learning
Polish and, hour after hour, for years
on end, Gombrowicz had been willing to teach
her a Polish that does not and never
did exist.

                    The man who told
the story would like to marry his girlfriend.
They love to read in bed and between
them speak three languages.
They laughed—at the wife, at Gombrowicz, it wasn't
clear, and I wasn't sure that they
themselves knew what was funny.

I wondered why the man had told
the story, and thought of the tricks
enclosure can play. A nod, or silence,
another nod, consent—or not, as a cloud
drifts beyond the scene and the two
stand pointing in different directions
at the very same empty sky.

                Even so, there was something
else about the story, like teaching
a stunt to an animal—a four-legged
creature might prance on two legs
or a two-legged creature might
fall onto four.

                I remembered,
then, the miscarriage, and before that
the months of waiting: like baskets filled
with bright shapes, the imagination
run wild. And then what arrived:
the event that was nothing, a mistaken idea,
a scrap of charred cloth, the enormous
present folding over the future,
like a wave overtaking
a grain of sand.

            There was a myth
I once knew about twins who spoke
a private language, though one
spoke only the truth and the other
only lies.
            The savior gets mixed
up with the traitor, but the traitor
stays as true to himself as a god.

All night the rain falls here, falls there,
and the creatures dream, or drown, in the lair.

Inscriptions for Gas Pump TVs

Midway the forest, certain,
parts its dark curtain.

～

Ride into the sunrise; the future
roars from the passing lane.

～

A dividing line binds the shook—
where are you going, gleaner?

～

Tears travel seaward. How
do you like their driving?

Piano Music for a Silent Movie

The gossips whisper their reproaches—
was it my fault I was too young for the war?

A muddy rain spoils every picnic,
but the fields are thirsty, the farmers are poor.

My talent lies in kissing and pretending,
and climbing barefoot up a trellis in the dark.

The neighbors are sharpening their pitchforks,
though no one dares to tell us. In the park

I found her note pinned to a linden,
her hair-ribbon snagged in a pine

—All the world worries a lover
when all the world seems like a sign.

I crossed the weedy river
and floated along to her door.

She promised me a portrait of the roses:
Forever Pearl, and Malakoff's Tour,

Gloire de Dijon, and Maréchal,
the Souvenir of Malmaison;

I promised her nothing but trouble—
my être had no raison.

Her hens pecked the grain from my pockets;
her cat ate the butterfat.

You needed a coupon for coffee, so I
brought her some cherries in my hat.

She stowed her watercolors in the rowboat—
I threw my books in the stern;

The oars dripped blue across our shoes
and we banked in a bed of ferns.

The crazy maid shattered the porch roof
while the merry-go-round never stopped.

Cannon pounded in the distance
(or was it thunder?)—every ear felt the pop.

As for us, we were always falling, deeper
than the tides and the moon,

Deeper than the quarry and the well,
and the shadows that hide at noon.

All this frenzy set the cocks a-crowing—
she let me choose a table and a chair,

The olive-wood glowed to embers:
she let me let down her hair.

"I kissed his ear and his elbow," she sang,
"and the silky side of his thigh.

I kissed his knees, I kissed his lips
and then he waved good-bye."

Our little spirit flitted,
as fast and light as a moth.

"Shameful," they said, "unlawful
—a troth, in the end, is a troth."

Love is a lapse and lovers liars,
the father weeps, the mother sighs.

The wagons are circling
below the bedroom floor.

One laughs too much,
the other cries.

The honeysuckle lost its honey
and the hens took their grain indoors.

Frost leveled the ferny banks
and ice grew thick on the oars.

I saw her face in the water.
I saw his face in the glass.

Some of us live in the present,
and some of us live in the past,

But it's the bootblacks marching toward the future
who trample the summer grass.

The gossips whisper their reproaches—
was it my fault I was too young for the war?

A muddy rain spoils every picnic,
but the fields are thirsty, the farmers are poor.

Atavistic Sonnet

Shadow of the gull on the airport wall, lunging

as the fuselage vaults above the meadow. Hollow in

the corn row where the hobo slept, then a backhoe

filling up the furrow. Misery of clocks in neon

glare, whereabouts of warblers and island foxes,

an old flame googled from the dead letter office—simple

as the still-warm bench at dusk. Typing or sewing,

or bringing down a fever through a length of knotted string

and a rusted staple gun. Here comes the tattooed

witch with her drum while the royals wait by the limousine

grinning. Shadow of the gull on the airport wall,

shallows in the stairs where we fell and stepped, hollow in the

corn row where the hobo slept, a backhoe filling the furrow.

Two Poems on the Name of Vermeer

toward the lake

Morning light, light at dusk, now
and then a step
from each other, the endless tuning of one string
against another.
Perfection in the first means the second
slips down
an entire key only to be keyed
up again,
and so on . . .
                    Light is patience and falls
in profile,
a pearl necklace strung by gradations
and the smallest,
at the moment of the clasp, rolls away
lost between
the floorboards forever, the strand left gaping
forever.
If I had a yellow dress and an open
window,
I am sure as much music could float in
on the wind
as could float out on the air,
and so on . . .
                    The great map
hangs above a leather chair studded
with silver rivets.
I can barely remember the word we use
for the map's crest,
that square that sets the ratio
and symbols.
It's posted there, obvious, and
oblivious to

the sea, but not of the sea, forever.
The fist of Spain
juts down, triangular.

I was happy there
in legend:
legendary sails of real
ships, a monster's
fins leaping, leaping past the beach,
a compass rose,
and so on . . .

from the lake

In the middle
of the night, to count up what is missing,
taking out
the wiry scale, holding it suspended like
a puppeteer
in a play about the ghost of nothing
chasing something.
Moonlight shines in on the scene.
A Last Judgment
looms from a frame on the wall.
Does allegory
then, start at the start, or come forward
on the glaze
of surfaces? In the middle of the watery
night, the plumb-
line snags in the eelgrass. The lecturer
said the name
meant coming and going, just the same,
though how
could that be true? You find yourself looking
for a clue.
You find yourself
looking for a clue. Why do
lost causes
always stretch toward the future when
the rest of them,
retreat, in silence, to the past? It's all
equivalence,
deferred. A set of substitutions.
A coin for all
the flecks that made the coin. Much farther south
the diver dreams

by lamps propped on the mast. The sea teems
with somethings chasing
nothings all around, and minor irritations,
iridescent.

Four Lack Songs

Alack Alas

Hammer to a copper bowl,
someone left the light on.
Touch against the thin wrist
skin, and back again, and back
again. Can't find the vein.

Alack A Day

Stiffing a filigree leaf, ribs
align in alternation. Drop
me a line, I am leaving—
the har-dee-har men come soon.
And once they are here, they are.

A Daisy

Soon the alterations are finished;
she mends where fray yields to fringe.
Wet thread creaks the slit like
chalk on a board. There's
no sense closing your ears.

Lackadaisical

You're just like the other, someone
said. I hear you, but where
are my shoes? I've looked every
where. I've looked high and low
and my feet are cold, and bare.

A Clown

"Avoid *then suddenly*" said the fiction
teacher, but some things do snap
into the field like my black coat
snatched all at once from my arm
as I crossed the Piazza Navona.

I was on my way to meet Brunella and Enzo
and had taken my route through the maze of alleys,
past the punks with their dogs by the Trilussa Fountain,

around the bollard and chain at the Ponte Sisto,
and down the slope of the Villa Giulia,

past the protesting Kurds by the Farnese bar
and the potted tulips in the Campo de' Fiori,
the leafy smoke wafting from the chestnut stand,

and the gauntlet of waiters flagging menus
near the immigrants hawking
their trolls and tin-can planes.

The Maya buskers were looping tangos
and I was running late past the living statues—
the knight errant and Cleopatra,
hurrying with my head down, my high heels
clicking, when suddenly, I was yanked back,
the coat ripped away,
a ripple of laughter behind me,
and, as I turned, there he was:
a clown,

hunched and wiggling, holding a black
coat—my coat—aloft, flapping
it up and down in the breeze
as he lunged,

mocking my surprise:
his red ball nose and stiff
black smile, too stiff
to smile, his face not a face, so
plaster hard above his waving
arms, his swaying torso, while
a silence, a sudden silence,
seemed to blast all through the piazza:

The frozen laughter of the tourists,
the waiters snapped to attention, standing
still, before the sound rushed back into
the vacuum, with a clatter of forks and knives.

Something dropped, a popped balloon,
and the clown going on and on,
composing his version
of the look of my annoyance,
a hip jutting out, an index
finger shaking "no!" as I stretched
to reach the tangled coat, then reached
and reached again
and he flicked it in and out
like a clumsy matador,
wagging his head, jiggling
his knee, spinning and circling
and feinting—his show.

How long it lasted, that panorama
of taunting, open mouths,
eyes squeezed tight over crooked teeth,
glasses tipping, plates clanking, by the thousands,
it seemed, and for hours and hours, when
just as suddenly he stopped

and threw the coat into my arms, tip-
toeing away to
find his next victim.

                  I turned and rushed
from the piazza, under the arch, and down
the Vicolo dell'Orso where Enzo and Brunella
were waiting for me. Flushed, I told
the story of what had happened: the sudden
hand, the waving coat,
the laughing crowd.
How in that preening dance the clown
had called up every ghost—
                        the divas and the ditzes, the ingénues
and mothers-in-law, the bimbos and sluts, the starlets
and clucks, the nerdy girls and little old ladies, the floozies,
the dogs, and the bricks—a parade that stretched back
as far as desperation, as far as the garden, as far
as the moon.
                  But as I spoke it came to me
like an image in a mirror
that rises to the surface

when the veil of steam
recedes, an image of the clown himself,
at dawn, in a mirror,
                  putting on
his rubber smile, his icy mask, his red
ball nose . . . a splintered shelf,
the pots of grease-paint by the sink
where he buttoned up
his polka-dotted smock,
pulled on his mountainous shoes.

A record stuck, an obsessive thought.
A sterile clown in a rented room.
Desert saint of drowned beginnings.
Refugee of a vanished rite.
Acolyte of envy or necessity.
The scapegoat's threat, the oldest fear.

        Who was he, and what
had he to do with me?
        The slow revelation
of a revelation made slower
        by surprise.

Meanwhile my friends still were waiting, and we were expected
on the other side of town, where we'd thought we might go to a show,
an opening, and maybe a reading after that—

the evening was early, the sky glowing rose, and plenty
of time left to decide.

"If you were one of the travelers, the guests"

If you were one of the travelers, the guests, who went down
to the ship that day, and you heard the band going

nowhere as it marched in place on the dock, and you felt
the lurching motion as the gangplank

was raised, and you saw, far below, the trash
on the water, oily and scattered, scattered

and sucked, by the cresting, ebbing, waves —
everyone waving, waving, before the window

rolled up again, a whining child, a whimpering
dog, a gull's scream in two-by-two-beat

gusts across the harbor, slowly resigned to
parting—turned away, while silence folded

over the deck, and the sky seemed as still as a sky
in a picture, you would not have heard then,

or in the days to come, the ringing shouts
of the stokers as they mined the stores of coal,

the banging pots and hissing steam that poured
from the kitchen and laundry, or the whispered

directions to the crew, for already the trio
would have struck its first C and you

would have leaned toward your partner just to
listen, while across the night, across

its barren field, the ship plowed a straight
path through the swell and the dancers

swayed and spun and turned to dreaming, as blank
as stars or winter . . .

stars and winter***^^^^^^^^***^^^^^^^^^
 **
             *
starless
         nights

         ()()() ()))) cloud, clouds

crossing moon ((()%

         crossing rain ^^^

rain in tendrils///crossing x x x

and windless days

winding
         -=-=-=-=into wind
^^^^^^^^^^^^^^^^^^^
**
         * blank fog

misting
                     starless

fog ## and mist

descending

the windlass
                     winding static

^^^^^^^^^^^^^^^^^^^^
sun^^^^ into^^^^ moon^^^^

    into haze^^^^^fading

———

then frantic

frenetic bluepeter

hoisted

      rust on the azimuth @@@
        circle

          whirled @

wheeling whirling
        unmanned

the prow inhuman prow

now foreign far

from touch or knowing

^^^^^^^^^^^^^^^^^^^^^
- - - - - - - - - - - - - - - -

where you had come from and where you were going
bleached by the sun and vanished,

a brackish taste, a high-pitched
whine, and a port crouching low in the harbor,

and when you awoke, you had landed, lost,
where black smoke poured from the chimneys

and the streets seemed to shudder from the clamor
of the hidden machines, a gull's scream piercing

high above a filthy clothesline, then
higher, fainter, fainter, and gone,

a child jerking a stiff-legged dog
back from an oil-slicked puddle

where the air was pitted with grit, and the water
laced with iron—what you said was met

with laughter; your papers, they told you, were good for
wrapping bread; you might as well throw

away your keys, and so you came under the new
regime and spent your nights sorting the hand-me-

downs and handbags, the plastic bracelets
and knock-off jeans, the paper trees

with their paper birds and the many-colored blankets
that would bed them, and you shouldered your wares

in towers bound with twine and made your way
each dawn to the distant station, packed in

with the others to the thundering city where
you'd spend your days pleading, then running

from the cops, then pleading more, wheedling
on the sidewalks and bridges, beaten by the hot

sun, the contempt of passers-by—a coin
thrown down as a final gesture, a coin that made

you scramble and a coin that vanished, the song
you sang for money and the song to pass the time,

for now you were the host, the one who calls
out: now you were the refugee.

The Knot

The problem was how to begin with the end
and then it turned out there were two ends:
the end within the continuing
that, continuing, enveloped
the end. You passed yourself
coming and going, went through
one loop, then another,
what was behind drawn
through at a
slide until
it rose
before you, sprung.
Tangle like a bramble,
like a rose. Start,
start again against
the tight-
ening. A knife
could give up
on patience, but you
were born among
the dull and
kind, who wait
for Spring, and
lightening
and lightning.

The dead inscribed, alphabetical, within

the address book that slips
inside my pocket . . .

~~215 73~~
~~2 6690~~
late bloomer, connoisseuse
of dregs, "you must cultivate
a *why not me?* attitude"
toward your work,
you said, and what
will bring your death.

~~44 [0] 18~~
~~99 810~~
~~252~~
always on fury's cusp:
"revolutions conceived
in the fields are not
the same as revo-
lutions conceived in
the cellar"—you're convening
a committee against
the committee, sending
up a sapling
through a rock.

~~610 61~~
~~78764~~
take out the marrow, put in the marrow,
save a life, save another life—
the slight slope, you thought, was better than
the rise, to be in a hurry somehow
childish, degrading.

@midway.uchicago.edu
a wisp of smile below a wisp of hair,
the high view from your ivory aerie:
we took a walk where sere grass
reached our shoulders. Hot words
a couple sent drifting over
the water: "what a waste, a waste
of time," you said, and shrugged.

802 36
2 3097
after the war bravery
lost its occasion, all
the jokes that were yours were
one by one replaced
by secrets.

916 98
1 5917
from the window seat of your usual flight back
and forth above the Rockies, you laid down
the colors in short brushstrokes,
following the round shadows the clouds cast
on the perfect squares of the plains.

631 76
5 3521
a great blue heron—your totem
I saw one this morning and thought how weird
to say "feathering an oar,"
and remembered your sail's quick

thuck-a-thuck-a-thuck. "The thing
I miss most is Nature,"
you said, "in the nature
of arguments these days."

~~771 25~~
~~9 9653~~
A life spent tending
to beasts then unspeakable
agony months
of agony mute
as the non-human world
as you turned and were
turned in strangers'
beds. And now your names
together on the cold stone face,
a veil draped over the pasture.

~~Paul Minnie Avenue~~
"I will never again suffer an
Eastern winter" or summer
blowing in on the laughter of fools.

~~802 24~~
7 ~~6007~~
in Paris, where you never were, a girl
with red hair halfway down her back
is reading a poem about your drunken father,
the drummer, aloud to a metronome's tock.

212 62
7 2866
an idea was better
than writing it down, but flagging
a taxi called for
manifestation, on tiptoe
legs akimbo, and a two-
fingered whistle, stark
and shrill as a swallow's—
now your bold face
has joined the death
masks you so admired
for their perfection.

24 Berry Cove
on the phone I heard the white
pines wind-
ing, curiosity
shining through
a bridled courtesy.

001 06
338 22
46 584
we followed the sound of the waterfall below
the sibyl's temple and knew from the sudden
humming that we'd found the very
spot where Cinzia
stood listening, while
Propertius called and
called her name—
and wouldn't answer.

smallest monument bound
in marble paper, torn
leather spine:

the number you have reached is not in service
"les miens" he used to say

these were once mine
these once were mine

Voice-over

      undergrowth in creak, creak
           guttural the quarreling squirrels

a deckle-edged Spring, three

      hollow rata-rata-rata
         woodpecker
              on the right,
on the left
        (or echo)

landscapes, thinking to sketch
them, concentrating

      a-rumph a-rumph the bullfrog
      grown now singular

close on particulars
that otherwise would not
exist. There is something

      where once the peepers
         sang chaos, mounting, heet
            heer heet heet heet heer

inherently sentimental about
the idea,

      heet heer heet
just a month ago

it's neither here nor there, but then
that's what it means

wheedle wheedle wheedle wheedle
sweet sweet meetcha

to draw your way
toward it—

      silent pair of finches
      just ahead,
      vanished gold

the basin-deep skunk cabbage
leaves brim-full
of yesterday's rain

      and the hissing
            geese, their wheezing breasts inflating

the grasses wound
around and through them

       while their green infant,
         phosphorescent-
           fuzzed, scrambles

sentimental, like a pressed
flower that will lose its color

          across the path. The smaller
       the being, the more pronounced

the plastic debris inert

   the silence.

That's the difference—the draped
dirty tangle of torn
grocery bags.

With an ear to the ground, even
beetles make a rumble

Inertness, irreducible,
growth grown impossible—

nattering
          tattered spare-
                    narrating
                    sparrows

the never of it.

                    caw-cawah caw-cawah caw-ca
          caw-cawah (the always,
mates for life)

and the effort to record
came forward in all

          hermit thrush
          cascade
                    first flex, then
                    lushest
                    spilling

its own plasticity,

                    hooweet weet weet weet weet
          hoo weet weet weetweet weet

the lifelike, plastic—taxidermic,
pure arsenic

        cheer cheer cheer cheer   *cheer*

though words, in
life, like
life, are like
water

First Idyll

A long strand of ivy wound round and round the lip
of a cup, a wooden cup carved from boxwood
that grew for a thousand years.
My cousin has a little goat, black
and white, with a delicate
hoof that looks like
onyx from a distance,
and like coal when
you come close
enough to touch it.

After the Mowing

I

The season of the cut and clear. The bales squared
in the distance, a hollow house, no windows or doors.

The *N*s of the fence posts, perforated shadows.
The cupped sky, inverted. A sense of limit

in parallel lines, with no convergence in
the distance. The local held fast beneath

a vastness. I thought of the struggle against the angel
and the struggle against a stump, for the deepest roots

go into sky and earth alike. What arms
and rods can pry them? Inaudible,

> *oh why*
> *do you ask my name?*

> > The smallest meet
> the fiercest teeth and claws
> with soft mouth and
> velvet paw.

Invisible, farther,
the ax against the grain, bounced back,
ringing, from the heartwood's iron.

II

The wind was coming from the east,

toward me, holding

each vertical lightly on

its leash. Then slowly

stillness,

      and a rustling,

the fence posts now

near enough

to touch.

      There at the top of each, a massed

            form of

(slick gradations, brown, black and gray

like wadded swathes of

    taffeta,

        creased and folded,

           tectonic,

                fanned, unfolding,

then stiffening, anamorphic)

quills and feathers

now snapped

out, awakened, doubled shapes awakened

      and change, changing,

         into the full sweep of wings

into lift and speed, the air already churning

        at their tips—

It seemed the earth, too, was tossing like the sea

        as the great hawks rose,

        a pair,

             and dipped, circled,

             climbed into

the high flow,

        the wind's

           road, gone,

as two,

each alone.

III

to the *N*th, like the truth of an ending
unskeined across the crust of the white field.
Though it happened only once, I
am sending the thought
of the thought
continuing.
                To return to
the field before the mowing.
When a goldfinch swayed
on a bluestem stalk,
and the wind and the sun
stirred the hay.

Field in Spring

Your eye moving

left to right across

the plowed lines

looking to touch down

on the first

shoots coming up

like a frieze

from the dark where

pale roots

and wood lice gorge

on mold.

Red haze atop

the far trees.

A two dot, then

a ten dot

ladybug. Within

the wind, a per

pendicular breeze.

Hold a mirror, horizontal,

to the rain. Now

the blurred repetition

of ruled lines, the faint

green, quickening,

the doubled tears.

Wake up.

The wind is not for seeing,

neither is the first

song, soon half-

way gone,

and the figures,

the figures are not waiting.

To see what is

in motion you must move.

from *Red Rover*
(2008)

The Owl

I thought somehow a piece of cloth was tossed
into the night, a piece of cloth that flew

up, then across, beyond the window.
A tablecloth or handkerchief, a knot

somehow unfolding, folded, pushing through
the thickness of the dark. I thought somehow

a piece of cloth was lost beyond the line—
released, although it seemed as if a knot

still hung, unfolding. Some human hand could not
have thrown that high, or lent such force to cloth,

and yet I knew no god would mind a square
of air so small. And still it moved and still

it swooped and disappeared beyond the pane.
The after-image went, a blot beyond

the icy glass. And, closer, there stood winter
grass so black it had no substance

until I looked again and saw it tipped
with brittle frost. An acre there (a common-

place), a line of trees, a line of stars.

So look it up: you'll find that you could lose
your sense of depth,

a leaf, a sheaf
of paper, pillow-

case, or heart-
shaped face,

a shrieking hiss,
like winds, like

death, all tangled
there in branches.

I called this poem "the owl,"
the name that, like a key, locked out the dark

and later let me close my book and sleep
a winter dream. And yet the truth remains

that I can't know just what I saw, and if
it comes each night, each dream, each star, or not

at all. It's not, it's never, evident
that waiting has no reason. The circuit of the world

belies the chaos of its forms—(the kind
of thing astronomers

look down to write
in books).

And, still, I thought a piece of cloth
had flown outside my window, or human hands

had freed a wing, or churning gods revealed
themselves, or, greater news, a northern owl,

a snowy owl descended.

Lavinium

I met the girl who held the flower and mirror
and the boy who sent his hoop up to the god.

Put away childish things they said, and stepped
into the future. They were made of baked earth,
their tenderness intact.

Robbers there had come and gone, come
and gone for years
like glass.

In locked cabinets, washed up:
a bone brooch, the sea's
furl, an iron fire-dog.

The hoop rolled down again,
clattering.

The girl awoke and set her flower
inside the mirror.

The boy cartwheeled
behind his hoop, end over
end, over

endless sand. We think of them.
They never think of us.
We think of them.

And the hard-hearted doll
repeated the lesson:

love's asymmetry is true,
they never think of you,

love's asymmetry is true
love's asymmetry is true

Games from Children

my mother's garden

I lost my copper key
in my mother's garden

I lost my silver knife
staring at a cloud

I found my wooden boat
hiding in the rushes

I found my wishing stone
hiding in my shoe

I lost my copper key
hiding in the rushes

I found my wooden boat
staring at a cloud

I lost my memory
when I learned to whistle

If you find my silver knife
hide it in a stone

shadowplay

I made a fist
and it grew two ears,

long ears with
a mumbling

mouth. Then
I opened my hand—

it grew
four feathers

and another hand
rose to meet it,

and two
thumbs made

a doubled
dove's beak,

curving and
nodding on

the windless
white: one four-

fingered wing
swinging out,

the other
feathering in—

blackbirds of my
bedroom wall

black birds
flying faster

than the arc
of headlights

emerging
from the road

beyond the
window, looming

and emptying
looming then

emptying
then looming

then emptying
the room of all its light.

tag

Before you touch me,
I will run.
If I touch you, you
must stop.
If I lose you, we
won't stop
and must run on
as two
forever.
Try to touch the larch's
bark, try
to call it home.
If you go beyond
the grass,
you'll have no
voice, you'll
have no one.
Beyond the grass
time stops—
try to touch
the larch's
bark, try
to touch me,
we can stop,
we can try
to call it home.

red rover

red rover, red rover,
let them come over,
red planet, red star,
attacking, attaching,
come over war against
love overcome, and come
over, red rover, let them
come over, pleaser, permitter,
decider, old teaser,
spirit moving
formless through the startled leaves.

                    come over come over
As you stood there, shouting and waiting, shouting and waiting,
                  over come over
                  your arms linked inside
                  come over come over
                  the long shadows,

you knew the other view would come in time,

                  and be like time, silent
                  and waiting—

                  though first your name

                  let your own name *come over*
                      would have to tack
                          across that no man's land
                between the lines

                and come over.

So when it came, in a chorus,
        sudden and strange, like
              an offering that drew you on
              with all its glitter,

it hardly seemed
it could be yours,

and you looked around to see
if someone else were meant.

But then you were running, running, toward them, struggling to break them or
reaching to join them.
In the end, it would turn out the same—exclusion, inclusion, small changes of
perspective.

        That was how
        you first met the god
        of permissions, who has no face
        or figure, who never
        lingers in
        our image.

            But you didn't know that yet.

              Someone
        would twist and fall crying

        the sun dropped
        vanished

a scraped dish
a screen door's slap

and one by one

fireflies

the mothers'
voices lighting

calling her name

come in

then his *come in*

and yours
at last

you knew at once

come in come in come

in and in

though soon
in a dream again

you were running
running toward them,
struggling and reaching
reaching beseeching

if you can
if you can't
by a hickory limb

the future came wearing
the look of the past

and a spirit roved restless through the shaken leaves.

Oil and Water

In your hand, a Roman votive
lamp—made of clay, like us.
Fire-floating, failing sail across
the oil, then puff,
then void.

The silent fire held back within
its well. Smallest light in dust,
the smell of baked
earth and
bread.

Run your hand
beneath the running water,
hold it to your
lips. A word can
slip through thirst

like a wafer, like
a crumb.
A burn is cured with ice,
which makes a burn
then burn.

I knew a girl who saved a gull from death.
She gathered up its feathers gummed in tar.
She brushed the pinions down
with a toothbrush dipped
in soap, and gently
ran the faucet
on the breast.

A whale knows oil and water
and a song. This knowledge
comes from rain
and fervent
passage.

They say that oil
and water do not mix,
but one is life below
the light and one
is votive fire.

A whale knows
this, as does
a gull, as
does a girl,
now humming.

This knowledge
comes from rain
and fervent
passage.

A whale knows oil and water
and a song.

Titus

It takes a while
to notice the star-
shaped blight
of white, flecked

red in the black
fur, a hard bite
there in the cat's
back, but it

can be inferred
from the effort
it costs him
to move first

stiffly, then
slipped like a
stripped gear
from the rug

to the sill to
the threshold
of the door
where he stops,

slinking back
from his own
motion, as if
the world there

hurts, and hurts
him—it's like
the pain the sun
brings after

a deep sleep,
at least that's
what we think,
but, too, it took

a while to notice any-
thing was wrong,
and then we
turned to stars

before we saw
the truth. And
in that time,
the time between

noticing him, the usual
cat in his usual
place on the edge
of things in

their usual places,
and noticing some-
thing terrible
had happened—

where were we,
and what do we over-
look when we say,
as we do,
that state is bliss?

Thoughts made of wood

harbor hermitage
like thrushes
twinning
hollowing grain
chaffed or
flying
a chain
a larkspur
chain or cello
hefting
a just-hatched
breathing
or bent twig
twining
branch and trunk
along runnelled
paths some
leaf-
lined paper
a sheet
a one-piece
spoon too
poor for
a bed
for newborns
in the dresser
drawer dreaming

When I'm crying, I'm not speaking

Barred back from the glare
gone gripped along
the rail run down
running from or
toward no matter
no mind never
hell for leather
scraped across
night's increment
torn from the sedge
the salvage
shorn at
the edge forlorn
forewarned
hefting waxed
breached waning
whine needling
half heard
then hearing
help wound in
the wind

When I'm speaking, I'm not crying

The personal is artificially political just as
the political is artificially personal.

War profiteering has many means, including
the sale of poems against war.

Those who destroy the garden and poison
the well think that streets
will be named for them in the future.

       When Aeneas, son of the goddess of love, strides out
            alone on the empty
                 field, so recklessly
                     to meet the radiant killer Achilles, it's not
                    Love, but the god of earthquakes,
            who takes pity
       and lifts him, just
       in time,
right off the earth.

Meeting with slaughter, the mind breaks into parts.
Salvation hides below us and entire.

Songs for Adam

Adam lay a-bounden, bounden in a bond

I-I-I am-m-m-m a-a-a
l-l-l-likeness
without l-l-likeness.
I r-r-r-rule
the s-s-s-sea and the air.
I n-n-named a fish
and a b-bird and a stem,
and a f-f-foal by
the s-s-s-side of a m-m-mare.

My tongue was heavy, too heavy to move.
My feet were bound by roots,
but I learned to open my mouth
and sing,
to open my mouth like a bell, like
a flower.

the names

What name shall I give to thee?
What name shall I compare to thee?

anise bee and *cherry*
dark and *egg* and *free*
ghost hand and *icicle*
jinx and *kiss* and *lea*
many none and *other*
pain question row
sadness tree unusual
verity and *woe*
x I signed,
a *yawn* and *zed,*
and then I went to bed.

What name shall I give to thee?
What name shall I compare to thee?

I saw the whale shed the waves,
I saw the hawk shed the rain,
and though I was never
born, the light came first
at the limit of my mind
and with my own eyes
I could see

how all things on earth
must turn
toward the light,
though the light
has no likeness
on earth.

the dream
(four thousand winters thought he not too long)

Winter dream so sore
inside me, breath sharp
under my rib, a bent
stalk frozen
fast to another, snapped
back and lifted away,

then snow on her lashes and hair—
no, sun and dew
on her lashes,
her hair,

and the flies
buzzing in the grain

and the bees
grazing by the leaf

and the sweet dove
moaning
in the arbor.

I lifted my head to hear.

I awoke and she stood
before me, staring.
I awoke
and it all was true.

I could come upon a footprint now,
or take a turn, or find the start,

a name for something
even if it wasn't
there, was not yet
here.

the cool of the evening

Do you know every herb and seed?
he asked as he walked in the cool of the evening

(This god has intent and direction,
he knows where he's going in the cool of the evening)

Would you like to stay in the garden?
he asked as he walked in the cool of the evening

(This god has the leisure and means
to walk out alone in the cool of the evening)

There are two trees, but only one is of good and evil.
There are two trees, but only one is in the midst of the garden.
There are two trees, but only one is the tree of life.
Cherubim guard the gate and a sword
hangs crashed, hangs flailing, in flames.

Do you follow the deed with a double regret?
he asked as he walked in the cool of the evening

(This god cannot hide if he is everywhere,
he gathers his thoughts in the cool of the evening)

Cover your face with your hands and run,
cover yourselves and run.

lullabye

ashes burrs and *candlelight*
darkness endless fire
going home in
joy, I thought,
kindness leaves me now
only pity questions
rain speeds the tear
you will veer and
wander, veer and
wander . . .

ashes burrs and candle-
light, darkness ends
in fire, going
home in joy,
we thought, though
rain now, rain and tear.

as clerkes find written in their book

A child of my right hand
walked among the sheep
and a child of my left hand
drove the plow—

they were brothers, sons
of the self-
same mother,
no two more alike

than each other, fraught
with the pain of too little
and too much, with the pain
of too much and too little.

The god chose meat
instead of fruit
and the child
of my left hand rose up

to kill the other,
the child of my left hand,
the farmer, slew his brother,
the shepherd, in fury.

The god chose meat
instead of fruit
and the earth was stained
forever—

stained with the pain
of too little and too late,
with the pain of too late
and too little.

When you sleep in your chair
by the firelight, when you wake
in the morning and hear
the geese returning,

think of the child,
your father,
who drove the plow,
and was driven to despair,

the despair of too much
and too little,
the despair of seasons,
too little and too late.

Think of the child,
your father,
think of the mother,
your child.

Gold and Soil

In the kingdom of the mad they mine
the earth, and the poorest of the poor
make the descent. The keepers of the coffers
keep the coffins, too, jangling as they strut
around the town.
                         Below they know
the demons of the pitch. They pray
each night to gods of flint and fire.
They fall down on their knees, and
sleep right on the ground, and wake
to bells that never see the light.
I knew a man who knew a bird
so well, the bird would come
to call him in the dawn.
He had a patch of land he scratched and fed
all day, all day until the bird sang in
the dark. The earth does not send up
its rule of law, its emissaries fume
and break apart. The bird dies first beneath
the ground, beneath
all roots, beneath all art.
Now tell me how this dream
arose, a mouth,
and came to me.

Elegy Against the Massacre at the Amish School in West Nickel Mines, Pennsylvania, Autumn 2006

Lena, Mary Liz, and Anna Mae
Marian, Naomi Rose
when time has stopped
where time has slowed
the horses wear the rain

Mary Liz, Anna Mae, Marian
Naomi Rose and Lena
the lanterns lit
at midday dark
pain's processional

Anna Mae, Marian, Naomi Rose
Lena, Mary Liz
innocence has no
argument, justice
returns in a leaf

Naomi Rose, Lena, and Mary Liz
Anna Mae and Marian
a girl is not a kind of girl
she knows her rhyme
she has her name

Lena, Naomi Rose, and Mary Liz
Marian and Anna Mae
zinnias mixed with cosmos,
lupins caught
in hay

Mary Liz, Lena, and Anna Mae
Marian, Naomi Rose
someone had a newborn
calf that died into the light,
and someone knew the night

Anna Mae, Mary Liz, and Marian
Lena and Naomi Rose
someone knew the night
holiness mere meaning
when someone knew the night

Marian, Anna Mae, Naomi
Rose, Mary Liz and Lena
the mad put on death's
mantle, the mad
on fire with shame

Naomi Rose, Marian and Lena
Anna Mae and Mary Liz
the mother of the god you knew
was reading in her chair
and down came interruption

Naomi Rose, Lena and Marian
Mary Liz and Anna Mae
down came endless care
visitation's presence
bookmarked in a book

Anna Mae, Naomi Rose and
Mary Liz, Lena and Marian
your names in stone
your footprints kept
in mud between the stalks

Marian, Anna Mae and Lena
Naomi Rose and Mary Liz
iron bells toss
the clouds at dusk
and elders turn away

Mary Liz, Marian, Naomi
Rose, Anna Mae and Lena
empty-handed, hold their cups
with lead seams
supplicant

Lena, Mary Liz and Anna
Mae, Marian, Naomi Rose
a length of serge
so plain, so plain
the morning grass turned down

Anna Mae, Mary Liz and Marian
Lena, Naomi Rose
when time has stopped
where time has slowed
the horses wear the rain

Wrens

their tumbling joy
decanted descanting
over cobble
stones in and out
of firethorn back
and forth to gingko
who knows
who will
ever know
what net
binds them
loosening
song?
I would not
lose them
could not lose
them know
if there's
another
place another
world another life
there must be wrens.

The Lost Colony

They never learned to tell
one bird from another, a shrub

from a weedy sapling,
or when the season had

forced a flower's bloom, not
even if a berry

had ripened into poison.
And yet they drew endless

distinctions between
colors and polish and

coarseness of weave,
and would not let

their daughters
marry out.

They didn't keep
their children, though they

gave them tests and fed
them. They were known

for meticulous records, for
trophies and peeling stars.

They burned things up
or wore them down, had ranks

and staff and lecterns,
machines that moved them

from place to place, bright
jewels and playing cards.

They were old when they could
have been young, and young

when they could have been old.
They left a strange word

in a tree—*croatoan*—
and a track in the dust of Mars.

In the Western World

the sun is charity

That day the sun bore down
so fiercely coming looked like going.
We strayed, strangers in a strange part of town,
lost, past body shops and laundromats, tailors sewing
woolen hems and buttons out of season. "I am a moth,"
I thought, "I need to find a pool or, at least, a shadowed
corner, cool, near stacks of cloth."
But you were in your element, which is the glowing
blaze of noon, blinding, wherever,
whenever, your mind burns hot with impatience.
A beggar staggered toward us, "for God's sake," swaying, fevered,
and you stopped in your tracks. The light was radiance.
I would have hurried on, but for you that was the terminus.
The damp dollars, quarters, pennies, emptied without a word.
And in return no thanks, no thanks to us, no end of sun.

a boy's voice

Sometimes I catch the sound
of a boy's voice—a scrape, a scraping there, in the doubts
between what's certain. A boy's voice, bound
deep to old griefs and wonder. No wonder its roots
are hidden. You find yourself beside yourself
like a wild thing crashing
through suburban thickets, arriving all at once, helpless,
in an over-stocked backyard. Asking
or answering are the usual routes; murmuring time,
so slight, then postponed. But the boy's voice
has its music, a mixture out of crickets, pine-
cones, stones, trinkets—muffled deep in lint. A boy
with all the hours in the world, and long days I never knew,
a boy come whistling, whispering: sorely, scraped, and true.

the window seat

"Take the window seat—insist," you insist,
and now at thirty-five thousand feet, what I see
is mineral death. A salt lake, a mountain's crest
shorn flat, dust, sand, sand, dust, not a single tree
where the pale roads pale into more dust, more sand
(a cloud now and then like a stray puff from a banned
cigarette). The whole scene a triumph of vacancy.
Those intrepid wagons that landed
on the moon had four wheels made of wood,
a canvas top, a gunny sack. Some ill-formed notion of good-
ness and happiness. Guns. A crow shot out of the air.
Even so, they measured as the crow flies and spoke of days from here,
and waited for the snow to melt—
always at a loss for words, the ones for what they felt.

the figure in the garden

I

In the garden nobody sees
we leaned in heart-shaped chairs
and dropped a twig or sprig to please
the small fish circling there. A garden, a care-

less place, though who knew where or when
the math of hedge and accident had met
its happy end. We parted, and our chairs then
leaned together where we left them. A nest

and anthill came alive the moment quiet entered.
Later I returned alone, still thinking of that light,
as if the air could save the hum of every word.
But someone sat, his back to me, along the edge of trees,

a stranger, usurper, unmoved and unmoving,
troubling the wind and leaves.

II

No demon, it seems to me now,
and not an angel. He was the one in time who wrecks time,
piling up mirrors in a heap on the floor. I know
his shadow and his walk. He has all the time
in the world to stalk us, though no
designs on us. Just time taken, taking. He's timed
his entrance to meet his exit.
Sleep now, here's a cup
and pillow.
I was dreaming of a meadow,
not a garden. I thought, I remembered, just now
how I was dreaming, not of a garden,
but of a meadow.
The wind was still blowing, and you waited at the window.

a little room

If you want to kiss in an elevator
you have to know when to start.
You can't begin to bend any later
than the third floor. Your heart
is pounding (and buttons are glowing,
which means someone's waiting,
though not for you). There'll be springing,
whistling, and sudden abating,
two, then one, then two. Intent, intended,
push > < and pull me into your arms,
close and closer, suspended
(the lock switched off alarm).
Above is looming, below's the abyss—
and meanwhile the **3** is the charm.

the rocks beneath the water

Today, wandering, I could see the rocks
beneath the water, the foundation,
for the creek was clear in the clear light. The great oaks
and laurels lined the bank, their station
permanent as earth. Everyone knows that time is water
and, deeper, knows that water
erodes away all stone. But today I knew it didn't matter,
rocks or creek, creek or rocks, the slow floods
of memory, then nothing, will endure.
I remembered you at that moment
and, flowing, all the hours of since and later, immersed
in something more than monument,
and less than water—consolation
there and, in the silence, desolation.

there is no natural death

In the *Iliad,* there is no natural death—
everything comes about by intent
as if the pulse and very breath
we take were something meant
to be shaped. All that violence
out of somebody's error.
The same clumsy butting against the sense
of things over and over, horrible,
then somehow forgettable. And in the middle of the shield,
in the middle of the day, in the middle of their never-
ending tasks, the women go on yielding
to it, scrubbing the corpse cloths whiter
than ever, digging with their sticks in the dirt,
hauling the water back and forth, over
and over, where it runs forever through the dry ditch.

moon at morning

Ghostly chalk rounded low in bluest
sky, seeing, while the gulls circle
inland—lost, you think, though they know,
they must, where they're going. The women
now pinning up their washing, a tin
basin, a caboose or a tugboat, forms
of future in the distance. Found,
you think, though you couldn't say exactly
where they are. There was a place where you
were walking, though now, and now, it's fading
—it's fading, will be gone by the time
you arrive. Love there persisting
when love has almost died, when the dark it knew
has died, and still it waits, the white conscience.

the fox

Did we live lightly then?
Twice we've seen the fox,
the flash
of red that leaps
the weeds and brush, an after-
image gray,

then blank, then gone
delight cannot be sought
or pleasure thought
or joy re-caught
but twice we saw the fox, not once,
and knew his fear of us

Step in time, love, step in time,
live inside the morning
twice we saw the fox, not once,
and knew his fear of us

The Field of Mars as a Meadow

They ran with torches through the emperor's
wheat field, setting it to blaze
with a smell of burning bread,
for burning bread smells like
baked earth, as you know, and
the reason was their simple hunger.
Others came with plows, to plow it under,
and others came with stones
to cobble it over, still others came
with asphalt and tar to glue
it down, and the reason was
their need for motion.
Slaves were paraded
in triumph, in chains, through
arches built to make enemies
bow, while potsherds
and bones were thrown
to the rest, and the reason
was their need
to show their power.
The armies, public and private alike,
marched side by side
for the sake of a line
and shining mail,
hailing, conceding.
They said it was only
practice—and that
served as well
for a reason.
They sent up gifts
to the helmeted god so no one
would be struck down
by friendly fire.
The model boats were launched
on the flooded square to sail

in and out between
the statues. Young boys came running,
shouting and whistling,
women leaned dizzily
from kitchen windows,
with shutters shoved back,
cheers filled the air,
confetti fell in everyone's hair.
How long ago that was
no one remembers.
Barbarians and pirates,
marauders and merchants, courtesans
and priests came and went.
The reason was the banks and
the cathedrals, and the sidereal
path of the wind.
The old streets curved into
hidden alleys, tapering
to stucco and dust.
The new ones were bulldozed
the width of tanks,
and squadrons of police
on horseback.
The reason was
to mind the mind of
the crowd, though
riots broke out in all
the piazzas. And the reason
for that was the banks,
or maybe just
the cathedrals.
When the revolution
finally ended, they
led in the cows, draped
with garlands of flowers.

Happy couples spread their picnics
here and there among the trees,
with punch and cake
to celebrate
the former age had ended.
By then my own country
started up along
a shore, impenetrable as
forests, deep
as forests.
Four walls were built
with a window facing
east, where the sun
disappeared on time
every morning,
and always returned
the next. Stories were told
in the winter dark—
of course the reason
was the need
for explanation.
Sages and prophets, as they
must, looked on ahead,
and said there would be
night before the dawn,
so they made another window,
larger, facing west,
and pushed the horizon
even farther in the distance.
The house grew lurching
wheels, and took to a road
made of sand and
mud, through
prairies and deserts and
mountains, all

the way to the sea.
Everywhere they went,
they left behind
a graveyard,
though the reason
was better left
unspoken.
Unspeakable now,
on the street below my window,
one boy is thinking of
killing another
over the five-dollar
bill that's flapping there
in his hand.
The first boy has a hidden
revolver. He found it
this morning beneath
his uncle's pillow. Or maybe
the gun found the boy.
The reason is hard to know.
Things beg to be used,
a switch tripped,
a chain hooked, a countersink
sunk into the head
of a nail.
There's a portrait on the five-spot,
a slightly cross-eyed man
(the better to have more than one
perspective), with thin lips
and large ears (the better to hear)
who looks askance each time
the bill is lifted
by the sooty
breath of the wind.
The man's the one who freed the slaves

who traveled north by stars,
who raised the generations
who raised the boys now
standing there, poised
between the not-yet
and an aftermath to come.
Floating around the emancipator's
picture are doodles and
letters, insignia and numbers,
the serial impressions of long-
gone thumbprints, specks
of lint and ink—
hieroglyphic.
A medallion hangs there
just to the left, and, inside,
an eagle smaller than a dime
spreads out his
outsized wings.
A braided wreath made
of laurel and wheat
makes a tiny trapeze below his claws
while he balances, clinging,
to his perch atop a shield.
Flip to the other side,
and, around the running border,
you'll find the design
of dart and egg and
dart and egg and dart and egg,
symbols of war and love for more than
two thousand years.
But no one told the boys to look,
or taught them how to glean
a sign, and no one sees them
standing there; the not-yet
still is waiting.

A dart, an eagle of the law.
An egg beside a sheaf of wheat.
Things beg to be used,
to be turned, and
the reasons to withdraw
are hard to know.

from *Columbarium*
(2003)

Sung from the generation of AIR

               or vacancy, what memory can sing

before there is memory

               a breath sent into being before

a being

        draws in and out

               its breath, in darkness

when being,

        confettied,

               is not yet mote

not beam

       not remnant of cloud;

               a thin thread of motion

gathering weight

       in weightless

               space.

               There loneliness

leaned into nothing

                                        fell into the world

and was the first

                             of all things

falling

                  toward falling.

                                      How the stillness turned

and whistled

              and the whistle

                            was in the wind—

and a pod,

                released and rattled,

                      flew spilled,

then filled with air

a part of air

              in urgency,

           a boundary made by bursting,

what we call

the winding of the wind.

The ear is a drum and cavern

that will not close against the world,

and so we build our houses

where the wind cannot enter at will

blow the house down

stall the ship

the wind,

our enemy,

runs toward us in the night

or withholds

at daybreak

for days

on end.

I woke to wonder

what if the wind were evil,

the force of an incessant pain

Unbind, unwind the four winds

                                        without them, no direction.

                    ————————

Yet air is the element most bearable   most bearable to every mortal thing.

                    ————————

the flight

snatched away, the paper lands flat at first,

clings to the cement; the smooth side friction-

-locked to the pitted surface for a second,

then lifted by a corner,

then swirling, then dipping,

flush against the steel of a car door,

then flying off toward a branch,
                                        snagged,

unsnagged, sailing

On one side the answers were traced so carefully

capitals and small letters, peaks and valleys,

a black pen tacking between the blue lines.

Forget the answers, and then the test, and then the paper,

and then the sidewalk, and then the tree, and then the sky—

this is the order of forgetting, the one you already know by heart;

it is neither evil nor good, as things are neither here nor there when they fly *whisper*

A whisper within an ordinary parting,
a sigh nesting in a word, it comes
inside another breeze, warmer, softly,
to touch your cheek or shoulder, lighting down
as down does and doesn't and does again.
What was it?
You will ask yourself and you will ask
again until asking itself is like
a caress, nothing then something
and nothing again there in the clear as day,
but something, something meant—
what was it?

the memory of happiness in a time of misery

Like starlings in winter the wind beating against their beating wings
   the air numb and mutely blank a whiteness
      tumbling the dead leaves they too
        whirled like dead leaves torqued
          one way then another for the sake
            of each other even in death joined
              by their scattered dovelike gliding
                two heads bowed above a page
                  the lamp sputtered flickered sparked
                  in the deafening silence
                    the ear is a drum a cavern
                      that will not close against
                        the voice of the beloved and
                        the eye has a door
                          that can bar a whirlwind
                            a sanctuary shut to its harm.
                            Scirocco hot dust breaking in the mouth
                          dumb the tongue mute to reason cause
                        an eye held open to see not seeing
                        furled the thought dried to powdery sense
                    one way then another for the sake
                  of each other even in death joined
              by mistaken heaven's playthings
            gods needless mindless of consequence
          three heads bowed above a page
        an olive stripped bare of its silver
        and a hill stripped bare of its tree
         barren random an iron lung
      bellowing a dark cup thrown
    into the flames
   draw a clearing around the heart
so it might breathe freely again

the survival of Icarus

My father saw the feathers on the waves and grieved
and hadn't heard the voice within the wind
that blew the wax back into form the way
the cold dawn shapes a candle's foam.
I had heard that voice before
in some far time beyond this place
and I think of it now as a living net,
though I do not know how it spans our world
or if it sings from its strings or its spaces.

listen

in a golden field alone

lone

the quick dust whirling

hirling

eyes burning

urning

burning tears. Where

ere

was the other? Gone

one

and unknowing, no one

ne

could answer, crying

rying

there in desolation

solation

forgotten

gotten

forsaken

saken

for pity

pity

forbear

be air

"I had a little dove"

I had a little dove
made of paper and string.
I pulled him along behind me—
he could not sing.

He was a made thing.
I made him by heart.
He did not sing at all
and that was all of his art.

Apple

If I could come back from the dead, I would come back
for an apple, and just for the first bite, the first
break, and the cold sweet grain
against the roof of the mouth, as plain
and clear as water.

Some apple names are almost forgotten
and the apples themselves are gone. The Smokehouse,
Winesap, and York Imperial, the striped
Summer Rambo and the Winter Banana, the little
Rome with its squat rotunda and the Pound apple

that pulled the boughs to the ground.
The Sheep's Nose with its three-pointed snout,
the Blue Pearmain, speckled and sugared.
Grimes Golden, Cortland, and Stayman.
If an apple's called Delicious, it's not.

Water has no substance
and soil has no shell,
sun is all process
and rain cannot rise.
The apple's core carries

a birth and a poison.
Stem and skin, and flesh,
and seed, the apple's name,
no matter, is work
and the work of death.

If you wait for the apple, you wait
for one ripe moment. And should
you sleep, or should you dream, or
should you stare too hard in the daylight
or come into the dark to see

what can't be seen, you will drop
from the edge, going over into
coarse, or rot, or damping off.
You will wake to yourself, regretful,
in a grove of papery leaves.

You need a hillside, a small and steady wind,
a killing frost, and, later, honeybees.
You need a shovel, and shears, and a ladder

and the balance to come back down again.
You will have fears of codling moths
and railroad worms, and aphids.

Scale and maggots and beetles
will come to do their undoing.
Forests will trap the air

and valleys will bend to gales—
cedars will bring on rust, so keep them
far in the distance. Paradise,

of course, was easy, but you and I live
in this world, and "the fruit of the tree
in the midst of the garden"

says nothing specific about apples;
the "apples of gold" in Proverbs
are probably oranges instead.

And so are the fruits
Milanion threw down:
an apple does not glitter.

If you're interested in immortality
it's best to plant a tree, and even
then you can't be sure that form

will last under weather.
The tree can break apart in a storm
or be torqued into pieces over many

years from the weight of its ruddy labor.
The state won't let you burn the wood
in the open air; the smoke is too dense

for breathing. But apple-wood
makes a lovely fire, with excellent
heat and aroma.

Fire will take in whatever it can
and heat will draw back
into earth. "Here is the fruit,
your reward and penalty
at once," said the god

to the waiting figures.
Unbearable, the world
that broke into time.
Unbearable, the just-born
certainty of distance.

You can roast late apples
in the ashes. You can run
them in slices on a stick.
You can turn the stem to
find the letter of your love

or chase them down with
your chin in a tub.
If you count the seeds to tell
the future, your heart will
sense more than your

tongue can say. A body
has a season, though
it may not know it,
and damage will bloom
in beauty's seed.

If I could come back from the dead, I would—
I'd come back for an apple,
and just for one bite, one break,
and the cold sweet grain on the tongue.
There is so little difference between

an apple and a kiss, between desire
and the taste of desire.
Anyone who tells you other-
wise is a liar, as bad
as a snake in the quiet grass.

You can watch out for the snake and the lie.
But the grass, the green green wave
of it, there below the shadows of the black
and twisted boughs, will not be
what you thought it would be.

Bees

That the bees were born in the corpse of the injured animal.
That the bees came forth out of the corrupted flesh.

That a small room was chosen, made narrow just for this,
and the animal was led beneath the low roof and cramped walls

and that the four winds came through the four windows
and that the morning fell upon the small

and heavy head, its horns curving out
from the whorled medallion of the forehead.

That the hot nostrils and the breathing mouth were stopped
and the flesh was beaten, pounded to a pulp,
beneath the unbroken hide.

        He lies on his side on the broken apple-boughs. He lies on a bed
      of fragrant thyme and the cassia is laid in sprays about him
and the sweetness of the fields surrounds him.

Do this when the west winds blow. Do this when the meadows
are alive with poppies. Do this when the swallow hangs her pendulous

nest and the dew is warm and the days grow long.
And all the living fluids will swirl within the hide, and the bones

will dissolve like bread in water.
And a being will be born, and another, and then a thousand

and a thousand thousand swarming without limbs or form.
And that the wings will grow from atoms. And that the stirring wings

will find their way into the air. And that a thousand stirring wings
will come forth into the day like a storm of arrows made of wind

and light. And the flesh will fall back into the earth, and the horror
into sweetness and the dark into the sun and the bees
thus born.

—Virgil, *Georgics,* Book IV.281-314

"Dark the star"

Dark the star
deep in the well,
bright in the still
and moving water,
still as the night
circling above
the circle of stones
the darkness surrounds.
Dark the wish
made on the star,
a true wish made
on the water's image.

There is no technique in the grass.
There is no technique in the rose.

Ellipse

Night after night the astronomer
    imagined the stars in their orbits,
        building his orrery of glass and string;

        he was making a kind of singing
    that came from far beyond
himself, beyond the sounds
    that human mouths will bring
        into a form of being.

        And then, one night,
    it came to him
that the circles and spheres
    had no meaning—that,
        spinning, the globe's center

        might not return, ever,
    to its point of beginning.
Instead a new circle
    was entwined there and
        another, and another—

        until each was traversed
    and described in its path.
It seemed to be the way the thread
    a silkworm drops is thrown
        around itself,

        building a kind of house from
    the weaving of so many
small orbits, drawn out
    from the center on one side
        and drawn in from the other,

                    producing an uneven motion,
          alternately fast and lingering.
It was late, and reading
          about the astronomer,
                    you thought grief could take

                    a shape like this. You thought
          a loop, placed, then displacing,
could wind around and around
          as each turn verged farther
                    from its start, plying its motion

                    without a given rhythm—all
          things following from diminishment,
all things following a weighted
          spin until you could not
                    bear to return to where

                    the loss, your loss, had been.
          While you sat reading, late
into the night, someone was
          setting a table, someone was
                    packing with slow precision.

                    The quiet metals— a fork, a spoon—
          lay on the snowy cloth.
Someone turned down the sound
          and it backed once more into silence.
                    Leaving your book, you came

                    into the room just as a door
          in the distance was closing;
the surface of the table,
          you realized, was still warm
                    from where a hand had been

resting. And you saw
how the room was like a clearing
in a forest; the brambles fell away
and the vault of sky appeared—the kind
of story you were told again

and again in the years before
you could read. You had half-
heard those words, like the thoughts
of someone sewing, or someone
compelled by bright flowers to

wander deeper
and deeper from
the road toward home.
You could not be more alone
in that place

that was the source
of all your forgetting.
And then you recalled how
the saint had said that
a body tends to follow

its own weight, its own weight
to its own place, not always
downward, not always toward
the earth, but to its own place
like fire rising upward.

If the lights of the heavens
were to cease, he said,
if the potter's wheel continued
to be turning, all things would go
to their own place and the sun

and the moon and the stars,
as well, would follow the time
of returning to their places,
the time that no one yet knows.
You came into a room that turned into

a clearing and the clearing bore
outward like an eye. Oil beneath
water rises over water; fire on
the water is carried upward.
Things in their order seem to be

at rest, but are moving toward
their places with an inner fire
and weight. You thought you
were singing the song of the orrery,
where all things follow the motion

of light. But the stars are perfect;
we do not live among them.
We do not know them and
cannot know them; their music
steals the senses

and slows us into sleep.
You were moving with a purpose,
though you did not know it yet.
You were moving like a sleeper
through the shoals

of night. And that is how you
found this place; you cradled
one ear against the sky and put the other
against the ground. You chose your form
of leaning: you chose to stop and fall.

Forms of Forts

hay fort

A labyrinth. A pencil shaft of light
wherever four bales couldn't squarely meet.
The twine tight, lifting as abrading.

A twinge, the prickly collar rubbing,
a scratching rash along the forearm.
The heaviness of the hay in the hot dark.

So earnestly, we set
to building for ourselves.
That there should be something
where before there was nothing.

Then the fervent hours
of catching and pretending,
the dreaming hours of strings
and lucky stones.

If you touch one of your hands
with another, the one that touches
will seem alive, the other like
an object to be awakened.

When winter ended,
the doors were rolled back and the broad day
flooded the loft.
And then we could see, in the swath

Of sunlight, the stray clover bud,
or jewelweed, or fireweed,
or evening primrose,
or robin's plantain,

Thistle or chicory,
even once great mullein—
the leaf that's called
velvet dock.

Whatever had been in the mower's path
was bound and pressed into the hay.

You cannot know both hands at once;
you must choose between the living and the dead.

A labyrinth broken open from above
or worn away at its foundations.

That there might be something where before there was nothing
and the source of light confused with holiness.

snow fort

Come in, come here, come into
this place that's been made for us,
that was packed and braced for us
against the collapsing rain.
Come in, it's a cavern in the white
heart of the sea. Come in
where the silence is like breathing
moonlight, where a faint taste
of iodine will lie on your lips
and you'll never be cold again.
In every part of space, there is another part of space.
When this is gone, it will not disappear.

"Let me tell you about my marvelous god"

Let me tell you about my marvelous god, how he hides in the hexagons
of the bees, how the drought that wrings its leather hands
above the world is of his making, as well as the rain in the quiet minutes
that leave only thoughts of rain.
An atom is working and working, an atom is working in deepest
night, then bursting like the farthest star; it is far
smaller than a pinprick, far smaller than a zero and it has no
will, no will toward us.
This is why the heart has paced and paced,
will pace and pace across the field where yarrow
was and now is dust. A leaf catches
in a bone. The burrow's shut by a tumbled clod
and the roots, upturned, are hot to the touch.
How my god is a feathered and whirling thing; you will singe your arm
when you pluck him from the air,
when you pluck him from that sky
where sorrow swirls, and you will burn again
throwing him back.

Two Brief Views of Hell

Leaving the fringe of light at the edge of the leaves, deep then deeper,
the rocking back and forth movement forward through the ever-narrowing circle
that never, in truth, narrowed beyond the bending going in,
not knowing whether a turn or an impasse would lie at the place
where the darkness turned into impenetrability, deep where
no longer could down or up or side to side be known, just the effort
to stay above the water, to keep one spread palm bearing
against the weight and then the other, deeper and deeper.
The way in was easy once it began. The way in was all necessity.
Behind the darkness, more darkness; beneath the water only water.

A great black frayed trash bag lifted by the wind high above the sidewalk,
then just above the roofs, a black shining sail tattered, too big to be flying
and yet, each time it began its descent, lifted, propped up
and stiffened again in a sequence of small swirling movements.
The most oppressive thing,
the most tormenting, a black sun deflated, teasing,
touching the cornices and windows, block after block,
a hovering force, a curse, a smear.
The farther it rose in the distance, the larger it seemed to loom.
The mind wants an object and then recoils at what it has done.

The mind wants an object and then recoils at what it has done.
The farther it rose in the distance, the larger it seemed to loom.
A hovering force, a curse, a smear,
touching the cornices and windows, block after block,
the most tormenting, a black sun deflated, teasing,
the most oppressive thing
and stiffened again in a sequence of small swirling movements
and yet, each time it began its descent, lifted, propped up
then just above the roofs, a black shining sail tattered, too big to be flying.
A great black frayed trash bag lifted by the wind high above the sidewalk.

Behind the darkness, more darkness; beneath the water only water.
The way in was easy once it began. The way in was all necessity
against the weight and then the other, deeper and deeper
to stay above the water, to keep one spread palm bearing
no longer could up or down or side to side be known, just the effort
where the darkness turned into impenetrability, deep where
not knowing whether a turn or an impasse would lie at the place
that never, in truth, narrowed beyond the bending going in,
the rocking back and forth movement forward through the ever-narrowing circle.
Leaving the fringe of light at the edge of the leaves, deep then deeper.

Kingfisher Carol

halcyon—a period of calm weather which exists during the seven days preceding and the seven days following the shortest day of the year; so called from a nautical tradition that the halcyon, or kingfisher, builds her nest on the water and that in spite of the violent weather prevalent at this time, the gods grant a respite from all storms while she hatches and rears her young.

Star for the shepherds,
star for the kings
and the kingfishers
perched on the waves.
On the halcyon sea,
they nest their nests
from twigs
and briars and hay.

Jars of myrrh
and silver caskets
locked with
golden keys,
eastern starlight
trailing eastward,
the manger
piled with sheaves.

Pelt and steam
in a timbered stable,
the kings fall on
their knees;
shepherds lean
on their staves to doze
and dream
of meadows and leas.

The light shines
there in the desert dark
and the darkness
knows it not,
shines on the flocks
and the towered walls,
on the throne
and the narrow cot.

Star for the kings,
star for the shepherds,
the kingfishers sing
from the waves.
On the halcyon sea,
they nest their nests
from twigs and briars
and hay.

The Rose

Not so long ago, or was it?—the bud was tightly wound and the edge
as hard to start as a roll of cellophane tape
      (though it wasn't up to you or me to start it)

Remember how the "dew and velvet" first caught our eye?
      how the butter-yellow striations went
            into pink, or withdrew from pink?

(though it wasn't up to you or me to say which way it was going)

The corolla did unfurl. The anther cracked and flew.
      Each part in fact played its part, and when we turned away,
            it didn't die—of course, or not
                  because of that.

Eventually, it shattered
      like any rose, just as roses do:
            first the outer
                  petals, then the inner ones that cling
                    a little longer
                        to the pistil,

though even that wasn't the end, for the hip
had hardly begun—its apple-green knob
would still take months
to ripen and wither

—the very months that send
      their filaments toward the sun:
            the *long ago,* the *start,*
                the *little longer, eventually,*
                    the *end* like clockwork—notions
            drawn from simple math, like *clockwork.*

When you and I are gone, it's true
that time will die in time.
It won't be up to the rose
to say which way
the wind has blown.

I was wandering alone in a ruin
as vast . . . as vast as the moon . . .
and thought that time
had a form of its own,
but then the rose came to save me.

Scarecrow

Now, when I picture him, I realize his secret
     was that he had no secret.

    The whole summer long he lived
        less than a life
            and more than the existence
                that is granted to objects.

    He resembled a place and a person at once,
        his getup first fit for a hoedown,

            then bleached by weeks of sun and rain
                until denim was done in, tattersall
                    fell into checkered tatters.

Under the straw hat, instead of a face,
    there was only the notion of a look,

      something steady, still,
        when all the living world

        knew fear as
           an atmosphere of presence.

        The sun at noon and the moon effaced by clouds, the wind
in the shocks and the light

    on the leaves, a mouse
nosing a chipped cob,
    a beetle climbing around a thorn—

these moved as if they were meant to move

while the crows,
        toward whom his being was bent, read

his immobility
      as a form of intention.

Hair-trigger,
        lime-twig, rusted
saw-tooth on a spring:

a crow's mind can never reach
      the point of not
         really minding.

He was a figure on a stick and the stick stuck
      in the ground; no one

         would have named him or offered
         any thanks—

         anthropomorphizing is what crows do.

The gods do not have bodies and souls;
      they have only their radiant bodies.

         They are perfect and have no sense
         of their perfection.

He couldn't slow or die, would not
      return to earth. Seedy, seeded
         he was scattered by the wind, scattered

helter-skelter
        by the raking wind.

We built his heir
        from the rag pile and the straw
            that fell from the loosened sheaves.

You don't have to believe to know
    how such a scene can happen:

    how nature depends
        upon its image of our errors

      and how we, in making what takes place
          in our absence, find some part of ourselves
             that does not grow.

Lost Rules of Usage

period
a tollbooth   a jammed F sharp
footprints leading onto rock

question
a noble brow above the missing lips

comma
red willow leaf
       suspended in the water
an eyelash gone astray on a cheek

colon
adhesive tape mending
       the bridge of your sunglasses

semicolon
a knot and a stain in the plywood
some people can't make up their minds

dash
might as well die trying

exclamation
the slim clown leaping over the ball
a strained expectation leading onto nothing

quotation
one week we slept like spoons in a drawer
       the next week, the same, but in the other direction

parentheses
the condemned man dreams of his pardon
what I think of when I do not think of you

Vigil

Midnight much worry
in a little room—
strike a match and time
is burning toward you.

Wings

If you could have wings would you want them?

      I don't know.

I mean, if you could use them to fly, would you want them?

      Yes, if I could fly.

But they would be really big.

      How big?

They might brush against your knees as you walked, or be bigger than some doorways.
      And what if you couldn't ever take them off?

      I still would want them.

If you couldn't take them off, even if you were going somewhere,
      or going to bed, or eating at a table, or you wanted to pick
      someone up, you could never take them off?

      Yes, I would. I would still want them.

Because you could fly?

      Yes, because of the flying.

And if they were heavy, or even if no one else had them, and even if
      your children and their children didn't have them?

      Yes, I think so.

But you would still have arms and hands and legs, and you could still
      speak, but you had wings, too. You would want the wings, too?

      Yes, I would want the wings, too.

And when you were walking around, people would stare at you, and they
    wouldn't necessarily understand that you could fly?

    I understand. I understand that they wouldn't understand.

Or if people thought they meant something, something they didn't really
    mean?

    I would know what the wings were for.

And if you had them, forever—the forever, I mean, that is your life,
    you would still want them?

    Yes, I would want them. I would take them, so long as I could fly.

that I might fly away
    that I might fly away where the ships
        that I might fly away where the ships of pine wood pass between the dark cliffs

from *The Forest*
(1995)

The Forest

You should lie down now and remember the forest,
for it is disappearing—
no, the truth is it is gone now
and so what details you can bring back
might have a kind of life.

Not the one you had hoped for, but a life
—you should lie down now and remember the forest—
nonetheless, you might call it "in the forest,"
no the truth is, it is gone now,
starting somewhere near the beginning, that edge,

Or instead the first layer, the place you remember
(not the one you had hoped for, but a life)
as if it were firm, underfoot, for that place is a sea,
nonetheless, you might call it "in the forest,"
which we can never drift above, we were there or we were not,

No surface, skimming. And blank in life, too,
or instead the first layer, the place you remember,
as layers fold in time, black humus there,
as if it were firm, underfoot, for that place is a sea,
like a light left hand descending, always on the same keys.

The flecked birds of the forest sing behind and before
no surface, skimming. And blank in life, too,
sing without a music where there cannot be an order,
as layers fold in time, black humus there,
where wide swatches of light slice between gray trunks,

Where the air has a texture of drying moss,
the flecked birds of the forest sing behind and before:
a musk from the mushrooms and scalloped molds.
They sing without a music where there cannot be an order,
though high in the dry leaves something does fall,

Nothing comes down to us here.
Where the air has a texture of drying moss,
(in that place where I was raised) the forest was tangled,
a musk from the mushrooms and scalloped molds,
tangled with brambles, soft-starred and moving, ferns

And the marred twines of cinquefoil, false strawberry, sumac—
nothing comes down to us here,
stained. A low branch swinging above a brook
in that place where I was raised, the forest was tangled,
and a cave just the width of shoulder blades.

You can understand what I am doing when I think of the entry—
and the marred twines of cinquefoil, false strawberry, sumac—
as a kind of limit. Sometimes I imagine us walking there
(. . . pokeberry, stained. A low branch swinging above a brook)
in a place that is something like a forest.

But perhaps the other kind, where the ground is covered
(you can understand what I am doing when I think of the entry)
by pliant green needles, there below the piney fronds,
a kind of limit. Sometimes I imagine us walking there.
And quickening below lie the sharp brown blades,

The disfiguring blackness, then the bulbed phosphorescence of the roots.
But perhaps the other kind, where the ground is covered,
so strangely alike and yet singular, too, below
the pliant green needles, the piney fronds.
Once we were lost in the forest, *so strangely alike and yet singular, too,*
but the truth is, it is, lost to us now.

Slaughter

1

Remembering the shot that seemed to burst with no
rebound (early November, a time when the light
had waxed, but verged on turning back),
I asked what had happened and how it was done,
for I had been reading the same story over
and over of the breakdown in the fullness of the world.
I finally realized that what I had hidden from
in those early years was exactly the knowledge
that had disappeared behind the given-
ness of all things to us now. I had thought
that the very sound of the shot had created the silence,
the denying silence, around it. And that the lack
of an aftermath had come to stand for the loss
of anything I might have then known.

They began with the tools, the good set
of knives, the curved one for skinning and the straight one
for cuts, and the whetstones, the steels, the cleavers
and bell scrapers, the saws and the hooks, the stunning
ax and the windlass. They told how God had wanted
meat and so Abraham went forth—resigned
to duty's technology; how some things must
be done when the season is upon us and
once begun, cannot be left uncompleted.
The animal should sleep, they said, and be given
only water—for three days before
the killing time. The stunning must be short,
exact—a blow or shot to the forehead at
the cross of an X between the horns and eyes.

2

Then the sticker stepped forward, "If you want my job, you must face
in the same direction as the animal and stretch its neck
as far as possible, then press with your foot against the jaw
and forelegs while you cut through the skin from the breastbone
to the throat—you'll see at last the wind-
pipe is exposed. Push with your shoe on the animal's
flank; the bleeding will flow most freely."
(In the wilderness a voice was burning
out of the thorn-struck bush and the stones.
God had in mind a supplement, turning
the scene against itself, and would make
what seemed at first beyond measure
something trivial, undone—a kind of swerve
like mercy, shielding us from closure.)

They explained the skinning must start with the head,
and that, very slowly, the knife should be traced
from the back of the poll to the nostril on the left,
just along the line of the eye. They said to skin
the side and a short distance down the neck
until the head would be up on its base at last and,
grasping the head by the lower jaw, unjoint
it at the atlas, then cut, and twist, and pull until
it falls away, for good, on the ground.
Some of this had to be said with gestures,
but none interrupted or argued the order.
With the straight knife one would sever
the tendons at the hock joint. The hind
legs would hang then, dangling free.

3

The dewclaws have no purpose, but are taken
as a marker for splitting to the hock,
across the taut back of the thigh, to within
a few inches of the cod. Then the hide
must be split from the middle of the belly
without disturbing the abdomen's shell
or the delicate thin fell membrane.
Each name was given by Adam in the garden
during the sultry, buzzing afternoons
after the world was whole. They warned me
that the blood spots must be wiped, and
wiped away, then wiped again with water and
a warm soft cloth. The person who does this task
must have a tender kind of attention

And must make sure no leaves or dust fall
into the tin tub where the water swirls.
The caul fat must be taken out with care.
Next someone strong should loosen the pelvis
and the windpipe, then saw and split them each,
leaving them exposed. The meaning of crucifixion
comes from display and disappearance,
for when is the material ever more resistant
than when it is contradicted? The animal had lolled,
and slept, and grazed in its given hours, then gone
to the killing floor where time was rent by pain.
"Look to the heavens," they said, "count the stars,"
and so allayed the terror of the cry.
Behind the stone, the tomb yawned, empty.

4

Later the old ones told me how
to build the tripod from timbers and
how to stretch a gas pipe between the tendons
and the shank bones. Broom-handle sticks
are tied to the rope ends, then worked, lodged
as levers, to raise and spread the legs.
One explained how the skinning must proceed
with the hoisting, another told how to sever
and withdraw the stiffening tail. Taking turns,
they went into the beating of the hide,
the working loose of the rectum, the severing,
in the final stages, of the glossy violet liver.
"Wash the liver and hang it to cool slowly;
wash the heart—hang it by the small end, too.

Keep the fat clustered against the tongue
and hang it up to drain, and cool, and dry.
Save the rest of the fat for soap and tallow.
Wash the stomach until it's perfectly clean and
the inner surface webbed with white. When the carcass
has been split down the center of the backbone,
the two halves should be pinned with a smooth
muslin shroud. They must stay this way
until morning so that the living heat
will disperse and the fresh cuts can be
cold, and cleanly made." Out of one
being a vastness; out of one task
the division of labor; out of one shot
the myriad silence: winter's gory fruit.

5

Now let us go back to the stunning,
to the meeting of a human and animal mind, let us
go back and begin again where the function
overwhelms all hesitation and seems like
an act of nature. But they were tired and had no time
for me; the immense weight of memory dragged up
and brought back into the present was, too, like a large
beast, beached and spoiled. I finally grasped
what had happened, how the real could not
be evoked except in a spell of longing for
the past or the mime that would be, after all,
another occasion for suffering.
There would be no more instruction,
no more, in the end, hand guiding the hand.

Cinder

We needed fire to make
the tongs and tongs to hold
us from the flame; we needed
ash to clean the cloth
and cloth to clean the ash's
stain; we needed stars
to find our way, to make
the light that blurred the stars;
we needed death to mark
an end, an end that time
in time could mend.
Born in love, the consequence—
born of love, the need.
Tell me, ravaged singer,
how the cinder bears the seed.

1936

Her mother is rolling cigars in the factory.
She is best of all, even perfect. She taps
the woody threads, immaculate, into the acrid
raw silk of the wrapping.
Best of all, she can do it without thinking or asking,
could do it while talking, but doesn't, ever.
And so she could never be the cackling
floor-boss or the foreman who stands there
tethered to the watch. She's in it, for good,
on the floor, for life, watching the strings
tucked into their casings, each brown bud
taut below her long white hands.
And just her one thought—this is my
machine—the shroud around the shadows.
You, genre painter, who finds in this beauty
and who, from this, would make an enduring thing,
or you who could build from this some plot strung
with ornaments, constructing a monument
at the site of its senselessness,
turn away, turn from the din and the dust,
and choose someone else—not her.

The Arbor 1937

A thousand bees were tensing
on the blueblack grapes and the daylight

seemed to thicken
with hum and juice and shadow

                              coming back
        there are two there, and the little one can't be more than five,

                    does all the talking, while the old woman's
                              steadiness is certain.
                         The air is still and hot
                    they've taken everything under the leaves.

The leaves ruffled coolly, the tendrils curled
like treble clefs

                         And so it must have been September,
                    the month of her birthday. In later years, then,
                         this would seem like another coming
                    forward into the world. But what turned later, turned
                         in its way from tragedy to cynicism, as if
              somehow the sweetness of the dead became unbearable
                    and a kind of hardness would be a stay against
                              denial—a steadiness
                         that might be its own inheritance, or
                         just a distraction from the real—

The cushioned lid was thrown back, open mouthed
from the basket; the clear drawers gaping

with flosses, spools, and thimbles.
The scissors had been forged

as spread-beaked storks
and were plugged by then

with crabgrass and the knotted ends
of threads

                              (a theatre of forgotten scenes:
                        on the boards small dots and crosses
                     that could be followed), but the point of beginning
                              is the difficulty.

The naked rag dolls splayed
their muslin limbs, while the newer

rubber girls lay stiffly, their blue eyes
forever snapped open.

Her grandmother had measured
each bust, waist and hips,

a ruff of pins held tightly
in her close-pursed lips.

                              to explain sewing, and the shell;
                                 the whole struggle
                        from two to three dimensions, from the mirror to the body

                        extended, for what is made must move with us—it's
                     not something entered into, but what is donned or assumed
                              only after a meticulous labor—the given, her gift;

At their feet spread all the quarter-moons
of bodices, facings, and skirts—pinked

from the collars and cuffs and hems
of otherwise vanished housedresses.

a burden, for whose willing is this—
what compels us to repeat ourselves, and to repeat
what we never intended?

This is all she can remember,
and when she remembers, it is in a certain
order, but the intention
frays, at an irrecoverable edge . . .

how the old woman rose from the crackling wicker chair
and sat down on the grass with a sudden ripe weight,

her look distracted, given up, as if
another needle had been lost in the dusky shadows.

And how she leaned back all at once
on the heavy lattice, with her eyes closed,

her hands slightly open on her lap.
So that the needle did slip, glinting

from her fingers, into the tangle
of grass and threads.

And then the last thing,
the part she can't forget—

the downy leaf that fell

from the grasp of the vines, a muted
green leaf exactly

the shape and size of a five-year-old's handprint

When I look for symmetry, I cannot turn to this world,
because what is known must be in movement to be true.
The metaphor is relentless, coming up with an ease

that denies all time and care.
. . . handprints in plaster, the date scratched
in with a nail, the constant measurement of palm

against palm, finger to finger, an encroachment
that nevertheless accomplishes
distance. I cannot recall it, but it comes

without effort, the way the foot hits a brake
and the right arm flails out, ready, able
to save what needs saving.

as if her own hand had floated

down so softly
to land on the cheek. And how it stayed there,

unspeakable—its fall and its stopping.
How it stayed there, fast,

as if the wind had ended,
as if the sky had been emptied
of its air and its heavens;

look to the end and
the start is gone;
to one side
and the other is lost

how it stayed there
                    until at last the parents came back at dusk, found,
          the two of them there,
                    beneath the humming arbor.

What comes back, comes back from another
place, and doesn't save us, but alters
and, even in denying us, can turn us.

I had asked for a third term, and it came
in time, and was time in the garment
of our recognition.

Holzweg

I took a long walk through the chestnuts, the truth
of the light of day just above me where one wing
was replaced by another, then halted—as if a key
had been barreled over and over, to no effect or closure
in its lock. I thought of the dead ends, the little alleys
leading to the Forum, regardless of the turn

or seeming intention I might have told myself. I turned
to convince myself I meant to there beneath the fevered, true
green wreath of the world with its glory alleluia
of chestnuts and light. It was as if I were stopped in the wing
of an endless building, a kind of ruin wound in leaves and close
by a collapsing path, the vines' creamy panicles

catching me in mid-thought with my pocketful of keys
on a rusting ring. It was always in Spring that I hoped to turn
away from myself, away from the inevitable closure
of feeling, hoping that some feeble maxim was the truth,
that what returns returns when least expected, winging
its way back through an open window, an allegory

where anyone might be the subject, if not the hero. What folly
to hope for so much. There among the keys
were keys to doors I couldn't remember. I could wring
a cloth of all its water, or complacently turn
a wheel from side to side, or try to find the truth
in a pack of cards or the crumbling leaves, close

there in the bottom of a cup. It was no use, looking for closure
before the world was ready to yield it up. Better to follow the allée
of chestnuts even if it ends in disease and extinction, the hard truth
waiting at the close of beauty. And if not beauty then the twisted keys
of what could be haltingly thought and known. This turn
to the future was of course "a kind of courage," a wing

beating forward through an overly dramatic storm. What was hard-wrung
was also comic, full of weddings and well-wrapped presents, closely
kept secrets bursting with confidence and swerving turns
of phrase—like the song that murmurs "follow, follow,"
swept up and impoverished by its own poor echoes in a key
unnecessarily sharp or flat. In truth,

there was wax, or maybe ice, weighting the wing, trash in the alley,
some blank contingency at the close of it all. Still, I rummaged for the key
to the end of the terrible sentence, a turn, a light, a face, a truth.

The Desert (1990–1993)

1

In the sense that the world is happened upon
      and noticed—just as one morning the children
            came into the garden where the sun had streamed
                  through the larches: a perfect cone. They stepped
                      inside and felt for edges in the air,
                          asking if they should go or stay,

As if they were the cause of what
      they had seen. They knew that to walk
            away would be to leave in mid-
                  sentence, to turn from some gesture
                      that seemed urgently felt, but opaque
                        as a forgotten language. They were caught

Then, between wonder and its guilt,
      the overbearing insistence of wonder
            when it seems the up-staging of joy.
                  And they knew that the light would not remain
                      forever, whether they stayed or turned away.
                      Day after day the same thought

Of the country—the enormous effort of waste
      and complicity mirrored in the old concerned
            clichés. The struggle against forgetting
                like a stream or hill eroding,
                    or a fissure spreading while
                      we sleep, for we imagine

The loss of nature only in terms
      of the nature now lost, so far
            from our imagining. When de Tocqueville
                wrote his "Fifteen Days in the Desert,"
                    he said, "the forest seemed so icy,
                      the shadows so somber, the solitude

So absolute," not knowing all
　　　　we could have made by now and that
　　　　　　　what could pass away from the earth
　　　　　　　　　would be the earth itself beyond
　　　　　　　　　　　its use. Spellbound, he thought
　　　　　　　　　　　　　of the desert as a kind of revolution

In which the vast and granular world
　　　　was falling into its own full future
　　　　　　and he could, unwittingly, and suddenly,
　　　　　　　　be at the apex of that minute collapse.
　　　　　　　　　　History was not a line, but a kind
　　　　　　　　　　　　of hourglass, turned upside down,

As if to time an egg, and infinitely
　　　　reversing its own small, steady
　　　　　　progress. (. . . a light that was a slow
　　　　　　　　uncovering, a cloth drawn back,
　　　　　　　　　　a lid before an eye—like a blessing
　　　　　　　　　　　　on the world, but who is the dreamer

To answer their question; the one who predicts
　　　　or the one who follows? The blasted tree
　　　　　　fell in the single field,
　　　　　　　　the charred bark and the root
　　　　　　　　　　lay tangled like a severed braid.)
　　　　　　　　　　　The traveler arrived

In a landscape that until then
　　　　he had only hoped for, something
　　　　　　he could imagine when confronted
　　　　　　　　by emptiness: here and there
　　　　　　　　　　a cactus, a snake, what might be predicted—
　　　　　　　　　　　drawn on the shed skin

Of the world, these would admit
    a surface. He wrote "they have nothing
        to fear from a scourge which is more formidable
        to republics than all these evils
            combined; namely, military glory . . ."
                The children had stood beneath a perfect

Cone of light, which seemed a gesture
    urgently made by a speaker now far
        in the distance. All day
        the same thought returned: a desert
            filled with things beyond use
                and a will receded. Lieutenants

And lieutenants of lieutenants
    drawing a sandy line, wanting
        to be used and of use.
        A small cot beneath an enormous
            sky: indifferent, mathematical, true.
                The abandoned blocks of apartments, the rubble

Strewn like dunes across the view,
    caverns where vast
        machines have been severed—
        the leaking suitcase, the turquoise glass
        around the pull toy. It's all
        spelled out in the new edition of

"The New Dark": sensation, true
    indifference to all that could be new.
        How can particulars serve us when
        all they evoke is the identity of surface,
            the analogy of form which undermines
                their history? The replacements arrive

On buses and carry sets of working
        papers. They intend no resemblance to the living
            or the dead, and no one can say
                what they dream. They have nothing
                    to fear from . . . an empty country,
                        but the fires burning in infinite regression,

The smoke refusing all shape and measure,
        the end of the long daylight of reason—
            all consequence as soon forgotten
                as the last moments of a revolution.
                    A prophet in a frock coat gazed
                        out into the desert, imagining

Stars as a system of justice,
        reciprocal, mathematical, true . . .
            That night I dreamed
                of Constantine's dream and how
                    in Piero's great fresco cycle
                        the Emperor's face between the white sheets

Is so absent and calm; his secretary drowsily
        listens as the flanking guards hold
            their conversation—there
                on the eve of what they picture
                    will be an exhausting and cruel disaster.
                      And how the angel, like an arrow, or wildly

Plummeting bird—torqued from a sky
        so simultaneously brilliant and dark
            that it, too, seems more
                miraculous than made—spreads from the swift
                  left wing a perfect net
                    of light and drapes it over the great

Red and golden cone of Constantine's
        tent. And then the two folds
                of light swell forward—one
                        of this world, and one so surely
                                not—toward us like a pulse, thus stopping
                                        time in time . . .

To know what might
        be prevented, to see the luminous
                intervention, ephemeral
                        and true as the morning
                                light cast
drifting through the branches.

2

I understood that there must have been
    a light like a slow uncovering, or a cloth
        drawn back with all the pomp of a blessing.
        There must have been a lid
            long before an eye, a device for seeing
                before there was seeing. And the way in which

It came can't be separated from what
    it is—like a matter to be worked
        through so work can begin. When a line
            recedes, it seems that time passes, regardless
                of beginning, edge, or end. And the seeming
                    is like an event to us, with all

The consequence of something intended. It's just
    that the shape is prior—and not to see it
        is not a failure or collapse of
        will or faith, but a kind
            of belatedness that calls and calls
                again, for care.

In the sense that the pulse of the heart
    beats before its being, and out
        of the first layers all
            the organs will slowly form—a head,
                barely perceptible, surrounds
                the start of the brain

And a gaping hole appears before
    the hungry, speaking mouth. Below,
        at the beginning, the pointed tail
        will sway and the forty
            blocks of bone will start to turn:
                vertebrae, brain, and backbone

Curving while the sooty eyes lie open
         like coins in the ivory skull.
                 Branchial arms and legs, gill-like
                         projections that become the lower
                                 jaw, the neck and face suspended
                                         in the amniotic sac:

What has motion becomes
         a name in motion, growing toward
                 an end it does not know.
                         Chorion and amnion,
                                 placenta, cord, and rib; dermis,
                                         epidermis, and the shell's

Filmy skin; sweat glands, sebaceous
         glands, and then the emergent surface—
                 downy with soft hairs swimming,
                         soft hairs wavering—
                                 from their follicle anchors.
                                         The hands begin as shapeless paddles,

Then fingers form and nerves spark,
         stranded, stringing out into brightness;
                 the cells of the eyes diverge.
                         Ragged halo, chorionic villi
                                 —jerk, swish, hiccup,
                                         flex and flower.

The forehead grows, the vessels of blood
         thread, visible, under transparent
                 skin. The nail beds rise,
                         the hands are shaped and find
                                 themselves, grasping like to like.
                                         The head turns, the face moves

And a gasping breath begins
        its sore, impenetrable
            singing. The hollow stalk
                emerges, the stalk-end
                    thickens and forms a sphere, meeting
                  the skin's interior.

It turns on itself,
        inward like a cup, and the base of the cup
            becomes the fundus; the covering skin
                becomes the retina. Inside the lens
                  begins to glisten. An iris
                    grows inward from the edges

Like a circle of reeds
        leaning toward the watery
            light, becoming light and darkness,
                then color, shape, and motion.
                  And from the embryo's thin skin
                    a hollow forms beside the hindbrain,

Then the inner ear and the outer
        ear, the hammer, anvil, and stirrup.
            They bring the hard pounding
                of the blood beyond touch,
                  to the place of beat and interval.

Now it hears and hears
        itself in the pounding
            of the other, and somersaults
                into being: the one with the fontanel,
                  the waxy vernix, the matted lanugo
                    and its whorled tattoos.

One who is touched,
      became touch and shape; who came
          into the light, became light
             and movement; who moved
                into sound, became the speaking silence;
                    sent into time, became time emerging.

          As the past increases, the future is diminished
        and fear assumes the features of love.

The Meadow

When he returned from the meadow he said
that all the high grasses, coming almost
to his shoulders, seemed to be dead and yet
were also like wheat—brown and yellow with
a kind of weaving at the crest—and so,
too, could be something that might be gathered.
Then he began to tell me about the game
all the other children had decided
to play, how hard it had been, for some were
wild rabbits and others *young foxes*
although they seemed alike there in the luster
cast by the brown-red sun. That day there was
no wind, at least not at first, and so he
explained that at the start he could see just
what was happening: if he could sense some
motion in the grass, and yet no wind stirred,
he could know "there was some form of life."
The teachers told about the tunnels where
the mice would spend November. Another
boy had found the caterpillar's carapace.
But he was unsure of the word: "was that it?"
He could not place it, but he pictured it
resembling a shell or shiny crust.
"The wind came up," and then it was no longer
possible to tell what was something live
and what was just the wind again—like
a hand in the long grass, he said, just as
the game was over. And then I asked him
about the charred apple tree and the starlings,
and how he avoided the thistle's needles,
and whether the old snow had stayed there long
between the timothy's shafts? (For that
is what I thought all the tall grasses must
have been.) But he said, "no, the snow had no
leaves to hold on to," as it did, of course,

when it fell in the forest that was there
in the distance. And he said that nothing
was alive now that wasn't the color
of grasses. He hadn't seen the tree or
bird or snow, was sure he hadn't seen them,
and he wondered what kind of meadow
I could be thinking of.

from *The Hive*
(1987)

Man Dancing with a Baby

Before balance, before counting, before
The record glistens and the needle slides,
Grating, into the overture, there is the end
Of weight, the leaning into nothing and then

A caught breath, the record listens, the needle slides
Over slowly, and all at once around us a woman's voice
Stretches weightless, leaning into nothing.
Like a clothesline, the taut chorus: oh, hilarious

Oh baby, all around us, over slowly, a woman's voice
Gathers above the pick me up, pick me up
And the desperate put, put me down. First the tightrope,
Then the light foot, and the taunting chorus

Pick me up, pick me up. Oh, oh baby.
The slippery floor shimmers and spins like a record while
The light is swinging footloose on its rope
Out of time. The shadows

Slip, shimmering black, and spin across the floor,
Then turn back and pick up again. Oh seedpod stuck for just
One moment on the cattail, out of time, out of shadows,
Downy cheek against a beard: oh scratches

On the record, oh baby, oh measure
Oh strange balance that grips us
On this side of the world.

Seven Bridges

Sometimes before I wake I see
an iron bridge reaching across a clear
line of tracks, a bridge that begins in blisters
and rust and arches away
into morning. Then I'm walking across
its sharp rails, and I feel its sway
and ripple, feel it like any inhuman thing

with a beginning and end and no middle.

Or it could be this bridge, half-drowned
in the Susquehanna, half-dead in the yellow water
and its pilings furred by moss. Then on the other

side, the devil bridge of Bagni di Lucca,
convulsing like an ingot in the blast
of a furnace before it lands belly-up
and steaming. Beyond that the false happiness

of the bridge to Camden or the six boards
nailed across the cow pasture's creek.
Downstream, the bridge I can't remember

like pairs of wings lifting over Mexico.

There always comes a point when I'm tired
of other sides and remember there was only
one bridge after all: the one by the olive oil plant
in Somerville, Massachusetts.
It made an eerie music in the wind,
though I never crossed it in the morning
or in the evening, either.

Consecration

The man in the yellow hard hat,
the one with the mask
across his nose and mouth,

pulls the lever that turns
the great arm of the crane up
and over and sideways

toward the earth;
then the wrecking ball
dangles crazily,

so delicately, like a silver fob
loosened from a waistcoat pocket:
shocking to see

the dust fly up and the timber
sail up, then so slowly
down, how the summer air

bristles with a hundred splinters
and the smallest is a splintered flame,
for it takes so many lengthening

erratic movements to tear away
what stands between the sidewalk
and the bell tower,

where the pigeons now rise
in grand indignant waves
at such poor timing, such

a deaf ear toward the music;
in this way the silence
between hand and lever is turned

into a ragged and sorely lifted
wing: the wrecking ball lurches
in a narrowing arc until only

the dust resists—the rest
comes down, story by story,
and is hauled off in flatbed trucks.

Meanwhile the pedestrians come
and go, now and then glancing
at their accurate watches.

Gradually, the dust
becomes the rose light
of autumn.

But one evening a woman
loses her way as she's
swept into a passing wave

of commuters and she
looks up toward the perfectly
empty rectangle

now hanging between
the rutted mud and the sky.
There along the sides

of the adjacent building,
like a set for a simple
elementary school play,

like the gestures of the dead
in her children's faces,
she sees the flowered paper

of her parents' bedroom,
the pink stripes leading
up the stairs to the attic,

and the outline of the claw-
footed bathtub, font
of the lost cathedral of childhood.

Fire Ceremony

A girl called out to her horse,
called out in the October night
when the storm had ended.
She called out, wandering
through the brittle fields
where the corn was still dry
above the soft mud and the pumpkins.

Called out in the October night,
the siren moaned slowly, then rose
to a wail, yet far away as if
in another story's kingdom;
her father running out in
half-zippered trousers, her mother
shrouded in a cotton housecoat.

When the storm had ended,
an orange light stained
the sky above the meadow,
for the fire leaped up
like a half-spoken word, turned
into a myth with no place
of beginning.

She called out, wandering
closer to the woods, following
the creek's silver thread.
It wound between the deep oaks
like the end of childhood,
the way a flaw had been woven
in her mother's dark hair.

Then through the brittle fields
the wind came rustling,
carrying an animal fear;
the black calf with his damp nose
now dusted by ashes,
a spindly goat crazy in the heat.
The wind came up on its charred wings

To where the corn was still a dry
and broken path and the sparks
were a string of Chinese lanterns
bobbing above the barn. By dawn
the scarecrows had gathered
on the hill—stick figures, the curious
irrelevant crowd.

Above the soft mud and the pumpkins,
she could hear the rising siren
of the dogs; her mother running out
with a hen below each arm,
then her father stepping back
below the spinning eye,
the four hoofs flying
through the open hayloft.

The Evening of Montale's Death

A green light trailed through the park at dusk
like a lantern slowly lifted
by a search party, but it was only

A fisherman starting out
to avenge some private grief.

Two by two, the couples hurried
into the inn with its dulled music of spoons
against linen. This was the first

Evening of autumn.
The dogwood smouldered at its edges;

Soon every shadow would be blazing
into the black winter rains.
This was the last summer evening; a mist fell

Softly on the benches and on the lightning-scarred faces
of the pines. What the sun had tried to make simple

The night was about to obscure.
Because out of that mist with its comings and goings,
its rich promise of darkness,

Rode all the particular errors of God:
the june bugs carrying their swollen bellies

On frail and pitiful wings, while above
the mulberry trees tried to hide
their aborted, patchwork leaves.

A pair of runners limped by, their arms twined
around each other, and a small woman

In a large winter coat dragged
her wheel-less bicycle beside them.
There was a Boy Scout troop whose marching

Song was in the fabulous alphabet of the deaf,
and a man who swore over and over

To himself that he would never again
go home. They all ran after the trailing
green light and toward the promise of winter,

Away from some sure place of beginning,
which one by one

They had neither remembered nor forgotten;
just as at dawn a search party
gathers in an open field

And a lantern is held up to each face
to be certain that nothing has changed.

In the Novel

He described her mouth as *full of ashes.*
So when he kissed her finally
he was thinking about ashes

and the blacker rim just below
the edge of the ashtray,
and the faint dark rim that outlined her lips,

and the lips themselves, at the limit
of another darkness, farther
and far more interior.

Then the way the red,
paling, just outside those lines
caught fire and the pages caught

soon after that. Slowly at first,
but then all at once
at the scalloped brown corners of each;

like the ruff of an offended and darkening bird,
extended, then folded
in on itself; multiple,

stiffening, gone.

Life on Other Planets

Campo de' Fiori

Nothing so heretical as dusk—
the softened flesh of the peaches giving way
under their split panne skins

and the sepals of the harvested
Madonna lilies beading with
a sudden, sexual honey;

things opening and closing by
foregone equations: the clock tower
or this boy's spilling accordion,

the shape of a quarter note emptied,
then full-measured, beside the glossy
olives and salt-silvered fish.

Here at the center of this zodiac
of plenty stands Bruno's statue
at the site of his burning,

his black cowl restored, the articulated
folds now stolid, cold;
the city's pith.

Yet nothing in this age so heretical
as dusk, washing over the square
with its simple confusions—

number, name, the shifted heavens,
now opening shadows, now closing flames.
For if there are flowers on this

paved earth, why not flowers
on another and others
in our likeness—fallen,

threshed, in a field in late September
and the field itself falling
through the near-guess of night.

The Map of the World Confused with Its Territory

In a drawer I found a map of the world,
folded into eighths and then once again
and each country bore the wrong name because
the map of the world is an orphanage.

The edges of the earth had a margin
as frayed as the hem of the falling night
and a crease moved down toward the center of
the earth, halving the identical stars.

Every river ran with its thin blue
brother out from the heart of a country:
there cedars twisted toward the southern sky
and reeds plumed eastward like an augur's pens.

No dates on the wrinkles of that broad face,
no slow grinding of mountains and sand, for—
all at once, like a knife on a whetstone—
the map of the world spoke in snakes and tongues.

The hard-topped roads of the western suburbs
and the distant lights of the capitol
each pull away from the yellowed beaches
and step into the lost sea of daybreak.

The map of the world is a canvas turning
away from the painter's ink-stained hands
while the pigments cake in their little glass
jars and the brushes grow stiff with forgetting.

There is no model, shy and half-undressed,
no open window and flickering lamp,
yet someone has left this sealed blue letter,
this gypsy's bandana on the darkening

Table, each corner held down by a conch
shell. What does the body remember at
dusk? That the palms of the hands are a map
of the world, erased and drawn again and

Again, then covered with rivers and earth.

At the Font of Aretusa

Some things cannot follow:
the charcoal mask smudged
around the red unblinking eye

And the starched white taffeta
feathers of the swan

As once more, ruffling, unfurling,
she turns in the peacock-blue water,
is turned on the current

With the slow precision of any
mythological subject.

Above a hundred unlucky copper coins
and the single wavering milfoil,
hidden now and then in the dense

Papyrus that fringes her three
small islands, she is seen

As a consequence, a coda, to a likely,
unlikely, story of lust and water,
separate, then violate

Through chasm and river and
reef, water alternately

Stained and clear, revising,
polluting, male and female;
flowing, spiraling still, then

Clouding, arriving
at last at this final clarity.

This salt spring, invented at the limit
of Ortygia, where a dozen happy couples
peer and turn and listen

On the last day of January,
1983, two days before the almond trees,

Starting in the west, are reported
to burst into their double
white flowers, all at once—

that is, not in sequence.

from *Yellow Stars and Ice*
(1981)

Letter Full of Blue Dresses

Now the long evenings begin.
Two Amish girls are running
on the far side of the meadow.
A milk bucket joins their arms,
splashes frost on the thistle weeds.
Their dresses wrap around
their legs like ancient bruises, once
blue, now purple and black. Each
braid slaps the wind's face,
each thin leg stabs the frost.
This porch is the edge of
the world; I am not lying
when I say that to step
off the end of a plank like this
is to walk into another life,
where the first snow could enter
my skin, where the blue rag
thawing beneath the plum tree
would be the body I stepped out
of this evening. The stars
glow above the hayloft like
buttons from a serge dress,
like the dress I wore the day
the calf was stillborn,
the night the lightning tore open
the shed. I wake up constantly
to the sound of soft lowing,
to a clatter of shells
on the kitchen linoleum.
Two crows were killed
last week, chasing stars through
my window. I carried their
bodies from the slate roof
to the plum tree, burying
them under the frost. Their

thin legs seemed to point in
every direction. I have never felt
so lost as I did that morning.
For an hour I watched the water
pour into the sink
as if it were sky pouring out of
the faucet, or the blue cloth
a magician can pull from the fire,
as cold and silky as night.
Let me count the blue dresses
before sleep, anything to keep
from dreaming of the snow,
falling on my bed as if
it were a meadow where
two girls carry a silver
milk-pail and the thistles
tear at their hems.
Blue dresses, step into me
as if I were frost, as if
the clothes that live beyond us
were more like veins than rags.
And the headlights that sweep
across the walls this evening
were somehow necessary,
somehow needed, by the two girls
running on the far side of the meadow,
their dark feathers, their ancient light.

The Countries Surrounding the Garden of Eden

Pison, where there is gold

First they took the cedars and the larches,
stripping away their needles,
pulling them out at the root,
and who would have known that their satin
and green could line our path like thorns?
Then they took the flowering figs and the maples,
the petals that filled the air with sweet wings
stung, in the end, our eyes and our hands.
At autumn's golden pitch
they came with their fire and their
sickles, and even the orchards
unclenched their fists, dropping their arms
into the crackling grass. And the things
that once grew as we grew,
now changed without changing,
like the sand and the wind.

Gihon, that compasseth the whole land

At the first frost we found
our sheep with strangled
hearts, lying on their backs
in the frozen clover, their eyes
wide open as if they were surprised
by a constellation auguring drought
or endless winter. The wolves
walked into the snow, like men who
have given up living without love;
cows would no longer let go
of their calves, hiding them deep
in the birch groves. Everywhere
the roads gave off their animal
cries, running toward the limits
of what we had thought was the world.
And the names of things as we knew them
would no longer bring them to us.

Hiddekel, that is it which goeth toward the east

It began with the wells, coughing
their last drops and the fish with
blistered scales that were
tossed up by the river.
We left each day with empty
nets and ropes, for
our bodies seemed to lose
their way home. Candles
and tallow disappeared from our
cupboards until every house
came to live in darkness. The night
lost its noises one by one and
the silence filled us with a fear
of glass and strangers. That spring
no salmon or swallows returned, and
the river moved restlessly under
its ice, like us, like magicians
who forgot what came next.

Euphrates

Then one day when the sea
was as still as the sky and
the horizon disappeared within
its own folds, when every
nest had been emptied and scattered
and brambles and cobwebs
tore at our faces, when
our plows and our wheels
lay broken in the dust and our
instruments were like mute
and obedient children, when
our children no longer spoke
our language and our own
tongues were like stones,
sharp against our lips,
we dreamed of a country
far up the river, where a man
and a woman stood naked
in a garden, their faces
naked of memory.

How the River Climbed into This Poem

It is raining across my forehead and down
       my nose and into my mouth
and it is raining on the roof and over
       the eyebrows of the house, catching now
and then in the gutter's upper lip. It is raining
       on my neighbors and on the stranger's
furtive looks, raining on the Baptist hymns
       of the broomseller and his little brother.
It is raining down the pole of the barbershop, too,
       and up the stripe on the back
of the highway. It is raining and raining on City Hall
       and the ambitions of lunch dates
and divorces, even raining on the river, on
       the swimming pools and showers, raining
like a faucet on the pond's icy cheeks.
       It is raining on forsythia raincoats
and on mattresses left sleeping in the garbage,
       raining a revenge on the hardware store
and scattering the zinnia and squash seeds. It is raining
       right now on the dogwood tree
behind the empty house on Berks Street, raining
       on the wallpaper rosebuds there
until everything bursts into bloom. It is raining
       on the Mennonite graveyard and on the
delicate cemeteries of Fishtown, raining on the names
       of the dead and the flamboyant pseudonyms
of the living. It is raining on the trashbag's
       shining skin and raining on the pigeon's
matted feathers, raining on the sweet potato pies
       and the golden earrings of the vendors.
It is raining pennies and cats and dogs from heaven
       and raining the history of the future. It is
raining the great floods of Johnstown and Noah
       while the ballet of accidents begins.

It is raining in great sobs and single tears and raining
    on the night shift's restless sleep, raining
through the haze of tomorrow afternoon and the languorous
    picnics of July. And then, as if
a baton had been lifted and not at all like lightning or
    thunder, it stops as soon as it's begun.

Four Questions Regarding the Dreams of Animals

1. Is it true that they dream?

It is true, for the spaces of night surround them with shape and purpose, like a warm hollow below the shoulders, or between the curve of thigh and belly.

The land itself can lie like this. Hence our understanding of giants.

The wind and the grass cry out to the arms of their sleep as the shore cries out, and buries its face in the bruised sea.

We all have heard barns and fences splintering against the dark with a weight that is more than wood.

The stars, too, bear witness. We can read their tails and claws as we would read the signs of our own dreams; a knot of sheets, scratches defining the edges of the body, the position of the legs upon waking.

The cage and the forest are as helpless in the night as a pair of open hands holding rain.

2. Do they dream of the past or of the future?

Think of the way a woman who wanders the roads could step into an empty farmhouse one afternoon and find a basket of eggs, some unopened letters, the pillowcases embroidered with initials that once were hers.

Think of her happiness as she sleeps in the daylilies; the air is always heaviest at the start of dusk.

Cows, for example, find each part of themselves traveling at a different rate of speed. Their bells call back to their burdened hearts the way a sparrow taunts an old hawk.

As far as the badger and the owl are concerned, the past is a silver trout circling in the ice. Each night he swims through their waking and makes his way back to the moon.

Clouds file through the dark like prisoners through an endless yard. Deer are made visible by their hunger.

I could also mention the hopes of common spiders: green thread sailing from an infinite spool, a web, a thin nest, a child dragging a white rope slowly through the sand.

3. Do they dream of this world or of another?

The prairie lies open like a vacant eye, blind to everything but the wind. From the tall grass the sky is an industrious map that bursts with rivers and cities. A black hawk waltzes against his clumsy wings, the buzzards grow bored with the dead.

A screendoor flapping idly on an August afternoon or a woman fanning herself in church; this is how the tails of snakes and cats keep time even in sleep.

There are sudden flashes of light to account for. Alligators, tormented by knots and vines, take these as a sign of grace. Eagles find solace in the far glow of towns, in the small yellow bulb a child keeps by his bed. The lightning that scars the horizon of the meadow is carried in the desperate gaze of foxes.

Have other skies fallen into this sky? All the evidence seems to say so.

Conspiracy of air, conspiracy of ice, the silver trout is thirsty for morning, the prairie dog shivers with sweat. Skeletons of gulls lie scattered on the dunes, their beaks still parted by whispering. These are the languages that fall beyond our hearing.

Imagine the way rain falls around a house at night, invisible to its sleepers. They do not dream of us.

4. How can we learn more?

This is all we will ever know.

The Summons

I call you friend from the tree houses and caves,
from the soft moss by the animal graveyard,
from dove's wing and dog's belly beneath,
and friend from the spruce at evening where
the swing and the wind are the same in the branches
and each whispers a name not its own, friend from
abandoned houses where an open suitcase
fills with rain and real birds peck the birds
from the wallpaper, friend even from this.
From the spaces between rooms I call you,
from songbooks full of wasps in the attic
and the pockets of your father's uniform, friend
from spent bullets and feathers. I call you with
the barber's clicking teeth as your first hair
falls to the floor. I call you with the tongue
of the lizard in the springhouse and the bull's tongue,
raw on the salt lick. I call you with the bugler's
lips, with the lips of your oldest beloved,
I call you from the drum of the factory where
the carpenters hammer their thumbs. I call
you from the barn's darkest corner with
the language of spiders and cats. I call you
with the last key of the dismantled piano, with
the whistle of the child who can't whistle and
the tambourine of the man who is deaf and
dumb. I call you friend from the mirrors
and rivers, from the deepest most solitary
silences of sleep.

The Delta Parade

Everything stops.
A con man on his way to Baltimore
smokes for three hours in the club car.
The porter slips out and calls his wife,
he has one dime left and he's almost
yelling. Somewhere south of York,
she thinks he said. The funeral
procession leaves its lights on
and out of this pure stubbornness
its batteries go dead.
The bank robber leans on his horn
in desperation while his partner
snaps the rubber bands around
the money. A band,
you can hear it up the river,
first like the new heart of the child on
your lap, then like an old moon
pulsing below your nails, or something
softly moving through your arms and
throat. Here,
press here, not just drums.
A clown is throwing caramels
at the porch rails, balloons
are bursting or sailing up the river.
The lucky trees, to be able
to stand that close. If we talk
too much, we'll surely miss it.

And at the still center
of summer it starts; cowboys ride out
of another life, old cars get up
from the dead and dance
like cripples hired out for a tent meeting.
Up and down the sidewalk, the town
sucks in its breath like a girl

taking short gasps just above her trumpet,
or a fire engine's horn, heaving
like a drowned man or a heat wave slapping
against the water tower, this afternoon
just like a parade. The sore-footed
ponies are loaded down with flags
and the library float says
"Immortal Shakespeare," says it
with carnations and the hides of roses,
says it with a jester and a princess
wearing wings.

And she stutters, but no one cares
or can hear her. Except for the man
on the unicycle who tips his top hat
to the crowd, who swears he will
follow her anywhere, who follows
the mayor and the city council, who
follows the tap dancing class and the Future
Farmers, the Lions Club and the Veterans
of Foreign Wars; who clasps a carnation
between his teeth and sways
back and forth like
a broken clock.

And then things begin again,
a car follows the man on the unicycle
and suddenly it's just another car,
a pair of dice dangling
from the rearview mirror, a woman
giving her breast to a child and another
child carefully peeling a crayon, then
slowly giving the peels to his
grandmother, who opens the big brass
clasps of her pocketbook and lets

the bright curls drop slowly
to the bottom
like confetti or a boy's first
haircut. Like a first yellow leaf
that fell when we weren't looking.
Because it's summer.

Yellow Stars and Ice

I am as far as the deepest sky between clouds
and you are as far as the deepest root and wound,
and I am as far as a train at evening,
as far as a whistle you can't hear or remember.
You are as far as an unimagined animal
who, frightened by everything, never appears.
I am as far as cicadas and locusts
and you are as far as the cleanest arrow
that has sewn the wind to the light on
the birch trees. I am as far as the sleep of rivers
that stains the deepest sky between clouds,
you are as far as invention, and I am as far as memory.

You are as far as a red-marbled stream
where children cut their feet on the stones
and cry out. And I am as far as their happy
mothers, bleaching new linen on the grass
and singing, "You are as far as another life,
as far as another life are you."
And I am as far as an infinite alphabet
made from yellow stars and ice,
and you are as far as the nails of the dead man,
as far as a sailor can see at midnight
when he's drunk and the moon is an empty cup,
and I am as far as invention, and you are as far as memory.

I am as far as the corners of a room where no one
has ever spoken, as far as the four lost corners
of the earth. And you are as far as the voices
of the dumb, as the broken limbs of saints and
soldiers, as the scarlet wing of the blackbird,
I am farther and farther away from you.
And you are as far as a horse without a rider
can run in six years, two months and five days.
I am as far as that rider, who rubs his eyes with

his blistered hands, who watches a ghost don his
jacket and boots and now stands naked in the road.
As far as the space between word and word,
as the heavy sleep of the perfectly loved
and the sirens of wars no one living can remember,
as far as this room, where no words have been spoken,
you are as far as invention, and I am as far as memory.

The Dedication of Sleep

Each night I fall asleep
in honor of the dead, in honor
of the green-shooted irises.

Here in the small and enormous
cup of night, my sleep spills
over like my hair on the pillow.
Or something more familiar,
the bloodstains of the moon.

The train of the dead crawls from Rome
to Arezzo with the slow-witted
innocence of a child. The train
of the dead is naked, naked
without kerchiefs or flags.

I fall asleep in honor of the rain,
in honor of the restlessness of leaves,
and a great stirring passes
over the earth; it is the music
of our forgetting.

The train of the dead leaves
on Wednesdays and hardly
ever returns.

Sleepwalkers, pay attention to this
sorrow, this honorable sorrow that
reads over my shoulder, that stands
in the shadow of every doorway
and seems to bear me no ill.

Where are the women who
throw up their skirts, their
red slips, their happy blindfolds?

In the train of the dead there
is no dancing, no wealth
and no beginning.

I fall asleep in honor of the living
rain and my sleep winds through
the mountains of night like
a terrible fugue of rivers.

It is the eyes that are swollen
at the end of sleep,
the bashful eyes against
the morning's striptease.

The train of the dead has a flute-
like whistle, a far whistle
and no silences.

If you open the windows in the train
of the dead, the air rushes in
then out with alarm.
If you turn back a corner of the earth,
it will cover its face with its hands.

The way a bride turns and fusses
with her long net veil,
this train takes up
her tracks behind her.

Each night I fall
asleep in honor of the flower
girls who scatter
the green-shooted irises.

And since I sleep with nothing
in my hands, since I sleep
inside this human egg,
this nest of eggs inside me,

the bits of mud eclipsing
the half moons of my nails
eclipse each startled eye, each
dedicated sleep.

Notes

"A Language": Witold Marian Gombrowicz (1904–1969)

"Piano Music for a Silent Movie" is a retelling of Raymond Radiguet's 1923 novel, *Le diable au corps.*

"Four Lack Songs" were set to music by Ben Goldberg for the guitarist Shahzad Ismaily.

"After the Mowing": Genesis 32:29

"Lavinium" is for Pietro Zullino.

"Titus" is for the Wood family, to whom Titus belongs.

"Songs for Adam": "Adam lay ybounden," "Four thousand winters . . . ," and "As clerkes find written," from the carol "Adam lay ybounden," British Library: Sloane mss. 2593, ff.10v-11. The song cycle was written as a commission from the Chicago Symphony Orchestra, with music composed by James Primosch.

"The Lost Colony": *croatoan,* Karen Ordahl Kupperman, *Roanoke: The Abandoned Colony,* Lanham, MD: Rowman & Littlefield, 2007, p. 127.

"there is no natural death" is for Allen Grossman, who first brought that fact to my attention.

"Sung from the generation of AIR": the situation of "the memory of happiness" section comes from Dante, *Inferno,* Canto V.

"Ellipse": descriptions of planetary motion taken from Johannes Kepler, *Epitome of Copernican Astronomy,* trans. C. G. Wallis, New York: Prometheus, 1995, and the metaphor of magnetic threads from William Gilbert, *De Magnete,* trans. P. Fleury Mottelay, New York: Dover, 1958; "the saint had said" section comes from Augustine of Hippo, *Confessions,* Book XIII.9, trans. R. S. Pine-Coffin, Harmondsworth, Middlesex: Penguin, 1961.

"Forms of Forts": on touching one hand with another, Maurice Merleau-Ponty, *Phenomenology of Perception,* London: Routledge, 1989, p. 315.

"Lost Rules of Usage": "strained expectation leading onto nothing," Immanuel Kant, *Critique of the Power of Judgment* 5:333, trans. Paul Guyer and Eric Matthews, Cambridge: Cambridge University Press, 2000.

"Wings": the final lines are from Euripides, *Andromache* 862-865, trans. Susan Stewart and Wesley D. Smith, Oxford: Oxford University Press, 2001.

"The Forest" was written for Ryszard Kapuściński, who suggested to me that a time may come when no one will remember the experience of a forest.

"The Desert (1990–1993)" includes quotations from William Wordsworth, "Ode: Intimations of Immortality from Recollections of Early Childhood"; Alexis de Tocqueville, "Quinze jours au désert," in *Correspondance et oeuvres posthumes.* ed. Gustave de Beaumont, Paris, 1866, pp. 175–258; and St. Augustine, *Confessions,* Book XI, trans. R. S. Pine-Coffin, 1961.

Acknowledgments

The following new poems in this book have been previously published, often in quite different form:

The Academy of American Poets (Poem-a-Day): "Field in Spring"

The Academy of American Poets (poets.org): "Four Lack Songs"

The American Poetry Review: "A Clown"

The Berlin Journal: "Atavistic Sonnet"

Boston Review: "Piano Music for a Silent Movie" and "The dead inscribed, alphabetical, within"

Der Tagesspiegel: "Atavistic Sonnet"

The Kenyon Review: "Two Poems on the Name of Vermeer"

Lyric: "The Knot"

The Nation: "Atavistic Sonnet"

The New Yorker: "First Idyll"

The Paris Review: "Pine" and "After the Mowing"

Poetry: "A Language"

Raritan: "If you were one of the travelers, the guests"

The Warwick Review: "Atavistic Sonnet" and "Voice-over"

"Pine" also appeared in *The Pushcart Prize XXXVIII,* 2014, ed. Bill Henderson.

"Inscriptions for Gas Pump TVs" was published as a pamphlet, Cambridge University, ed. Rod Mengham and John Kinsella, 2011.

Susan Stewart is a poet, critic, and translator. She is the author of five previous books of poems, including *Red Rover* and *Columbarium,* winner of the National Book Critics Circle Award. She also has written six books of criticism, including *The Poet's Freedom: A Notebook on Making, Poetry and the Fate of the Senses,* which received the Phi Beta Kappa Christian Gauss Award, and *On Longing.* A former Chancellor of the Academy of American Poets, Stewart is a MacArthur Fellow, a Guggenheim Fellow, a Berlin Prize Fellow of the American Academy in Berlin, and a member of the American Academy of Arts and Sciences. In 2009 she received an Academy Award in Literature from the American Academy of Arts and Letters. Her poems have been widely published in the United States, England, and Italy, and have been translated into Italian, French, German, and Chinese. She often has collaborated with contemporary artists and composers—most recently with Ann Hamilton, Sandro Chia, James Primosch, and the Network for New Music. Stewart teaches at Princeton University, where she is the Avalon Foundation University Professor in the Humanities, and lives in Philadelphia and Princeton.

This book is made possible through a partnership with the College of Saint Benedict, and honors the legacy of S. Mariella Gable, a distinguished teacher at the College.

Previous titles in this series include:

Loverboy by Victoria Redel
The House on Eccles Road by Judith Kitchen
One Vacant Chair by Joe Coomer
The Weatherman by Clint McCown
Collected Poems by Jane Kenyon
Variations on the Theme of an African Dictatorship by Nuruddin Farah:
      Sweet and Sour Milk
      Sardines
      Close Sesame
Duende by Tracy K. Smith
All of It Singing: New and Selected Poems by Linda Gregg
The Art of Syntax: Rhythm of Thought, Rhythm of Song by Ellen Bryant Voigt
How to Escape from a Leper Colony by Tiphanie Yanique
One Day I Will Write About This Place by Binyavanga Wainaina
The Convert: A Tale of Exile and Extremism by Deborah Baker
On Sal Mal Lane by Ru Freeman
Citizen: An American Lyric by Claudia Rankine
On Immunity: An Inoculation by Eula Biss

Support for this series has been provided by the Manitou Fund as part of the Warner Reading Program.

The text of *Cinder: New and Selected Poems* is set in Adobe Garamond Pro. Book design by Ann Sudmeier. Composition by Bookmobile Design and Digital Publisher Services, Minneapolis, Minnesota. Manufactured by Versa Press on acid-free, 30 percent post-consumer wastepaper.